The Holy Spirit and Contemporary Man

The Holy Spirit and Contemporary Man

by Wayne E. Oates

BAKER BOOK HOUSE
Grand Rapids, Michigan

Formerly published under the title,
The Holy Spirit in Five Worlds
© 1968 by Wayne E. Oates
Library of Congress Catalog
Card Number: 68-11489
Reprinted 1974 by
Baker Book House

ISBN: 0-8010-6657-3

PHOTOLITHOPRINTED BY CUSHING - MALLOY, INC.
ANN ARBOR, MICHIGAN, UNITED STATES OF AMERICA
1974

To
the faculty of
The Southern Baptist Theological Seminary

Preface

Ours is a mind-restricted, inarticulate, and religion-rejecting era. "God-talk" is out. Speaking of God in a secular fashion is in. Yet the depths of men's being have merely translated, not erased, the moving letters of religious experience being written daily as the human documents of men's true being.

The purpose of these pages is to explore the subtle and obvious workings of the Holy Spirit in the religious experience of contemporary man as an individual. This is, however, an age of administration. Many churchmen have given up on the organizations and structures of the church. Yet, this very act of surrender is itself a form of religious experience. A fresh look at the work of the Holy Spirit in administration may speak to our desperation with the structures of the church.

The book moves from the vague but lively nebulae atmosphere of "the expanded consciousness" to the hard, obdurate, and bony structures of an age of administration. The living organism of the religious fellowship moves on a continuum between vitality and form, freedom and structure, creation and conservation. The chapters of this book are arranged somewhat along this continuum.

The faculty of The Southern Baptist Theological Seminary considerately invited me to deliver the Norton Lectures of 1967. No higher honor has ever come to me than to be invited by my fellow faculty members to present this study of the Holy Spirit and contemporary religious experience. The Norton Lectures, endowed by the late George Norton of Louisville, Kentucky, are supposed to explore the relationships between science and philosophy, on the one hand, and religion, on the other.

I am indebted to many persons for the kind of freedom of enquiry and utterance provided me by the students, the faculty, the trustees, and the denomination comprising the life and support of The Southern Baptist Theological Seminary. I am obliged to Professor Swan Haworth, Chaplain John Boyle, Chaplain Clarence Barton, and the graduate students in the Department of the Psychology of Religion—Richard Hester, Andrew Lester, William Arnold, Boyd McLocklin, and Franklin Duncan—for the consistent teamwork of a hard-working department. The seminars, the colloquia, and the research conferences provided the atmosphere of enquiry out of which these lectures have emerged.

I am also indebted to the staff of the Norton Memorial Psychiatric Unit for the privilege of participation in the understanding and treatment of emotionally disturbed persons, as well as to those disturbed persons themselves as they grapple with the issues of life and death. And finally, I have relied heavily upon the disciplined sense of perfection of my secretary and research assistant, Mrs. Richard Landon, as she has helped me both to gather materials and to edit the manuscript as well as to type and proofread the copy.

This volume is dedicated to the faculty and administration of The Southern Baptist Theological Seminary, who accept me as I am and inspire me to become something better each day.

WAYNE E. OATES

Louisville, Kentucky

Contents

The Holy Spirit and Contemporary Man

(1)

The Holy Spirit and the
Expansion of Consciousness

Professor Oscar Cullmann recently stated that Christian theologians have taken little note of a doctrine of redemption in Christ which includes the animal and the inanimate world. Schweitzer's reverence-for-life principle and some of the older sacramental systems of Christendom are exceptions to this. However, in the main, Professor Cullmann's estimate is prevailingly true. Not only does our doctrine of redemption exclude the animal and inanimate world; it also excludes great portions of the human being. We usually think of these excluded portions of our being as "the unconscious," as our "animal nature," as our "not-me," as our "worst self." We deify the rational; we think of the irrational as alien to our humanity. Our inveterate Western dependence upon Aristotle by way of Thomas Aquinas blinds us to great portions of our own beings as human beings. We consider much of our beings as persons as less than human and probably less than animal. These dimensions of our existence have been narrowed out of our consciousness. We are left with an entruncated and pinpointed kind of self-awareness which is insufficient for meeting the complex demands of our life today.

Consciousness-Expanding Drugs

The neglect of the wider reaches of consciousness has been forced into our attention by the recent experiments of many with consciousness-expanding drugs. Much publicity has even focused the populace's attention on the possibility of a wider view and experience of human life. At the outset, therefore, a careful review of some of these findings will provide a fresh, contemporary background upon which to focus an appreciation of the Holy Spirit today.

Professor Huston Smith of Massachusetts Institute of Technology speaks of the religious meaning of the consciousness-expanding drugs—mescaline, psilocybin, and lysergic acid diethylamid. These drugs do not knock out consciousness, but leave it operative. "They activate areas of the brain that normally lie below its threshold of awareness."[1] They dilate consciousness much like atropin dilates the pupils of the eyes. In fact, under the influence of the so-called psychedelic, or consciousness-expanding, drugs, the eyes are actually dilated. Contrary to this, opiates and other sedatives tend to decrease awareness of surroundings and bodily processes.

These observations of Professors Cullmann and Smith are reminiscent of a comment of William James:

. . . our normal waking consciousness . . . is but one special type of consciousness, whilst all about it, parted from it by the filmiest of screens, there lie potential forms of consciousness entirely different. . . . No account of the universe in its totality can be final which leaves these . . . disregarded.

How to regard them is the question—for they are so discontinuous with ordinary consciousness.[2]

Hardly less prophetic than William James' words in 1902 are those of Gardner Murphy, research psychologist at Menninger Clinic, uttered in 1947:

In a future psychology of personality there will surely be a place for directly grappling with the question of man's response to the cosmos, his sense of unity with it, the nature of his aesthetic demands upon it, and his feelings of loneliness or of consummation in his contemplation of it. There may be a touch of neurotic phobia in the persistence with which the modern study of man has evaded the question of his need in some way to come to terms with the cosmos as a whole. . . . Our study of man must include the study of his response to the cosmos of which he is a reflection.[3]

Walter N. Pahnke, M.D., devised a double-blind experiment, administering psilocybin to half the subjects and a semi-placebo to the other half. (The twenty subjects were chosen from graduate student volunteers at a denominational seminary.) An adequate set of religious atmosphere and setting of a chapel was provided for the experiment. ("Set and setting" refer to the physical environment and *planned* stimuli *around* the person taking a drug; a chapel, music, poetry are examples.) An immediate post-drug questionnaire, a follow-up questionnaire, and a content analysis of written accounts were administered after the experience. Nine criteria of genuine mystical consciousness drawn from a study of classical mystical writings were used as measuring continua for the kind of experience the persons had: (1) internal and external unity within oneself and with one's environment; (2) objectivity and reality in the direct experience at a nonrational level of the essential nature of existence both of the world and of oneself; (3) transcendence of space and time, which gives a person a perspective of the timeless in life; (4) the sense of sacredness, or a nonrational, intuitive, hushed, competent response in the presence of inspiring realities (this is similar to Rudolf Otto's idea of the *mysterium tremendum*); (5) deeply felt positive mood focused upon joy, love, blessedness, and peace; (6) paradoxicality, or the transcendence of the laws of Aristotelian logic by "feeling out of the body" while still being "in the body"; (7) ineffability, or the incapacity to condense any of one's experiences into words without distorting them by rendering them finite and impure; (8) transiency, or the temporary duration of the mystical consciousness as compared with usual experience; (9) positive changes in attitude or behavior resulting in the increase of trust and warmth toward others, a sense of relatedness with others, and a relaxation of the habitual mechanisms of ego defense.

In all these experiences, Pahnke found statistically important elevations of the mystical consciousness in the life of the subjects who did receive the psilocybin as over against those who did not. The sense of deeply felt positive moods of joy, blessedness, and peace were expressed as love on a very human level, but not as love of God. The sense of reverence or sacredness was awe in the pure sense of the word without being directed toward God per se. The most persistent positive changes were in the development of a distinct philosophy of life, the knowledge of a new dimension and depth in life, and an increased sense of the preciousness of life. There was more sensitivity and authenticity with other people and a relaxation of phoniness and callousness. The most striking single phenomenon was the conception of a death-birth experience, of having died to an old life and been born to a new, which gave a lasting sense of new significance and meaning to life.

In commenting upon the significance of the consciousness-expanding drugs with his experimental group, Pahnke emphasized that the drug alone was not sufficient. One cannot expect positive experiences automatically. He said that a meaningful religious setting and the framework within which to derive the meaning and integration of the experience was absolutely essential. Then, in the same vein of challenge set forth by William James and Gardner Murphy earlier, Pahnke said:

. . . the psilocybin experience might illuminate the dynamics and significance of worship. . . . Theologians must evaluate the light that such research could shed upon the doctrine of incarnation, the Holy Spirit, the presence of Christ, and of *gratia activa*.[4]

The "Drug" Challenge of the Holy Spirit

Sidney Cohen, M.D., and Keith S. Ditman, M.D., have clinically studied the negative effects of the same drugs. Interestingly enough, they refer to them as not only "psychedelic" (which means mind-manifesting and is a somewhat nonjudgmental term), but also as "hallucinogenetic" or "psychotomimetic" drugs. By this they mean that the results of these drugs tend to mimic psychotic states. Cohen and Ditman point to the following possible ill effects of LSD treatments: First, they "can produce a psychotic break, presumably by releasing overwhelming conflictual material which cannot be handled by the patient's established defenses"; second, they can "disrupt

psychic homeostatic mechanisms and permit reinforce-
ment of latent delusional or paranoid ideas"; third, they
can release pre-existing antisocial trends with acting out of
behavior and abandonment of social responsibilities.
Cohen and Ditman call attention to the black market of
these drugs in this country, and the complications of
prolonged psychotic reactions, depressive and anxiety
states, or intensified sociopathic behavior after unsupervised and inexpert use of them.[5] Similarly, Pahnke recog-
nizes the inevitability that illegal use of these drugs without psychiatric screening, preparation, supervision, and
follow-up therapy will lead to psychiatric casualties of
prolonged psychosis, irrational behavior, or suicide. Even
if the end result of an unsupervised use of these drugs is to
get the person who needs psychiatric treatment to such
help, "this is a risk-filled method of self-diagnosis," says
Pahnke.[6]

The Need for the Expansion of Consciousness

In the face of wide publicity and much misuse of
psychedelic drugs for the expansion of consciousness and
the realization of a mystical experience, the Christian
pastor and theologian today is given cause for thought and
prompted to ask, "What is it today that narrows the consciousness of people to such a great degree that they
would go to such desperate means to 'deepen and widen'
their spiritual lives?" Only passing attention is given to
this in the literature on these drugs. Primary attention is
needed. Most of the people who have received these
experiences have come from a "non-mystical background"
of conventional church life and have moved through the
nature and nurture approaches to Christian life and educa-

tion with little or no widening of their consciousness, traumatic or dramatic self-encounter, or discovery of the inner world. Middle class conformity to religion as the expected thing to do has inoculated them against "being fanatical about religion" or "reporting intimations of immortality" which they experience.

Furthermore, the classical means of inducing deeper religious experience are not a part of the Western Protestant tradition. For example, fasting is largely a secular activity motivated by the need to wear last year's clothes comfortably and by vanity to retain one's youth: we diet; we do not fast and meditate on a rooftop someplace in communion with the Holy Spirit. Neither do we have dreams and visions of "the heaven opened and something descending, like a great sheet, let down by four corners upon the earth." This was the experience the Apostle Peter had when he saw all kinds of animals and reptiles and birds of the air, and was invited to kill and eat. When he refused he was told that God had cleansed this, and what God had cleansed he must not make common. Nor do we have time to stop when we have such an experience and ponder it as did Simon Peter. Therefore, the Spirit does not speak to us and give us guidance as it did the Apostle Peter.

The "Drugless" Expansion of Consciousness

Today we are caught between the "far-awayness" of such experiences as that of the Apostle Peter and the "way out" experience of the LSD enthusiast. Yet right at hand are some disciplines available to every person but neglected by most. These seemingly mundane experiences have been associated with the experience of earlier participants in the life of the Holy Spirit.

Sleep deprivation and sensory deprivation such as the medieval mystics experienced tend to open the consciousness to wider ranges of reality. These rituals can be a part of life today and often are. Breathing and posture rituals such as are characteristic of Hindus and Buddhists open the consciousness to wider perception. But even though the Spirit of God is spoken of as the Breath of Life itself, we do not give attention to the regulation of our breathing or have such rituals as the Eastern religions do. But more profoundly than this, as Erik Erikson says, there is need for psychic space in the life of young persons who need a time of shiftless *Wanderschaft* or a psychological moratorium before they make the "ever narrowing selections of personal, occupational, sexual, and ideological commitments."[7] Spafford Ackerly calls this "a lying fallow period of consolidation" before entering into the frictions of realistic living. He says:

Something is needed before playing for keeps—before making these major life commitments, something very germane to the growing up process at this particular time. It is another period of play only this time with intellectual concepts holding off closure or solidification in any particular direction.[8]

But today the draft does not permit this. Although the armed services provide autonomy from "momism" and "popism" for young men today, they nevertheless substitute another kind of dependency in the place of parents. Decisions are made *for* the person. He learns to respect authority, but has every opportunity to expect others to *decide for* him. An Abraham Lincoln could sit with uninterrupted thoughts, free day after day to turn and look into himself. Goethe, failing in his studies at Leipzig, said that he could do nothing except love, suffer, dream, loaf, and let his spirit grow. Darwin failed in medicine and embarked on a sea trip aboard the *Beagle*. "His eyes were freed for the unexplored details in nature."

It was the Holy Spirit that led Jesus for forty days into the wilderness, where he was tempted by the Devil. He ate nothing, and was hungry. Kaleidoscopically all the issues of his life swept before him and the deposit of the psalmists and the prophets came welling up from within.

Class Competition and the Constriction of Consciousness

Probably the most devastating constriction of our consciousness today, however, comes through the anxious narrowing of our lives into castes and roles. The lower classes are afflicted with caste constriction, and the middle and upper classes are constricted by professional roles. These roles are "played," and each has his "part" as "teacher," "pastor," "doctor," "lawyer," "businessman," "administrator."

We can perceive ourselves as selves in at least two distinct ways: first, as a "part" we are to take in life, a "role" we are to play, an "office" we are to fulfill. A person thus is seen as "a composition of roles as well as a biologic, however unique and distinctive his personal patterning of these roles and his private value orientations toward the patterning may be." A second way of perceiving ourselves as selves is primarily an existential one: The self is a "being," even apart from his roles, with a personal participation in "life values internal to the person."[9] Drug experiences enable persons to "break out" of these roles. Richard P. Marsh, a college professor, participated in an

LSD experience administered by a physician. The physician himself was also under LSD. Marsh says:

The author . . . remembers . . . staring at the physician who had administered the drug with awed and liberating awareness that the man was no more a doctor than he himself was a professor. Both the "professor" and the "doctor," although duly certificated by the proper authorities, were, it appeared, manifestly frauds. What's more the discovery proved liberating and refreshing in the extreme. Two game players, one hiding behind the doctor role, and the other playing at being a professor, had come out from their costumes, abandoned the game, and, thanks to LSD, now sat confronting each other in a condition of headlong and naked reality. The feeling of lightness and release was incredible.[10]

Contemporary transactional approaches to psychotherapy have laid bare the way in which roles, games, and superficial pastimes are used to keep people at a distance, avoiding the demands of intimacy, and removing the threat of closeness, warmth, and tenderness. Eric Berne not only has done substantial research in transactional analysis but has made the substance of this research dependably available to great masses of people in his book *Games People Play*.[11] By way of commentary one could say that the Apostle Paul must have been terrified by the experience of seeing Stephen die. He saw Stephen as he, "full of the Holy Spirit, gazed into heaven and saw the glory of God, and Jesus standing at the right hand of God. . . ." Yet the murderers of Stephen laid their garments at the feet of Paul, then known as Saul, as they rushed together upon Stephen. In spite of this, Paul still felt that he must play the "game" of the Sanhedrin. He himself later sought to murder the disciples of the Lord Jesus Christ. But an expansion of his consciousness happened as he was shaken from the social armor of his role as a representative of the high priest. He experienced both visual and auditory revelations, which those about him could not see or hear. He was instructed to go to a man of prayer named Ananias, who in turn was instructed to accept him. As they met, Paul received his sight and was "filled with the Holy Spirit." My own interpretation is that this kind of opening of the spirit of man to the reality of God is possible when and as he is shaken loose and becomes able to transcend or break out from his role confinement. In pastoral counseling the "widths of perception" are not really experienced until a level of trust and security is established in Christ at such depth that "There is neither Jew nor Greek, there is neither slave nor free, there is neither male nor female [and, one might add, neither counselor nor counselee]; for you are all one in Christ Jesus" (Galatians 3:28).

By way of summary, I have said that the expansion of consciousness can take place today *without* the use of drugs. The "drugless expansion of consciousness" is hindered by the absence or decline of the great rituals of deprivation of food, such as fasting, the lack of the discipline in resting, sleeping, and breathing habits that characterizes some of the Oriental religions. Further constriction of the perception of reality is caused by the loss of adequate psychological moratoria from the fretful plunge toward adulthood, especially in preadolescence. Larger attention has been given to the way in which class competition and social "role" binding tend to imprison the spirit of man and prevent the larger perception of reality. These restrictions can be loosened by conscious attention and discipline. They often are broken by circumstance and necessity. Incursions of the larger reality and hope of God happen without managed planning on our part.

These, very sketchily set forth, are a few of the things

which constrict the consciousness and call for an opening or an expansion of the consciousness if religious experience in its depths is to come into being. I quite agree with Huston Smith when he says that while "religion cannot be equated with religious experiences, neither can it long survive their absence."[12]

The Christian Experience of the Holy Spirit and the Psychedelic Drug Experience Contrasted

What then are the differences between the Christian's experience of the Holy Spirit and the mystical opening of consciousness through psychedelic drugs?

First, both presuppose a "set and setting" of a community of faith. However, the Christian experience of the Holy Spirit arises from a clearly defined community of faith in Jesus Christ as Lord. The psychedelic experience at its most controlled and responsible level was found experimentally to be characterized by a vague, undifferentiated, and undefined sense of awe. This was not focused upon God, however. The most striking phenomenon was the sense of death and rebirth which issued in a lasting sense of new significance and meaning to life.[13] However, the Christian experience of the Holy Spirit itself becomes specious and untested when separated from the prior encounter with Christ in his death, burial, and resurrection.

The community of faith may express its identity through various symbolic foods and drugs. These become ornamental and ceremonial with an agreed-upon, non-controversial, and carefully interpreted meaning. They become symbols for instruction of the young and for renewed commitment for the older generation.

However, as Harold Fallding has said, a drug—be it alcohol, psilocybin, mescaline, or LSD-25—cannot create a community of durability and widespread understanding. Writing in *The Quarterly Journal of Studies on Alcohol,* Fallding speaks as a social scientist of "the eclipse of community among us," and says that "nothing could be less sufficient for the genesis of community than to supply the materials by which it would be symbolized if present."[14]

The account in the Book of Acts of the creation of the Christian community says it took place through the gift of the Holy Spirit to those who had attested to the resurrection of Christ. In Galatians freedom from constriction of the law and access to the fruit of the Spirit—love, joy, peace (those mentioned specifically by Pahnke in the psilocybin experiment)—are brought about by the Spirit as an aftermath of having been crucified with Christ, in spite of which one has new life.

The "set and setting" (the use of a chapel, religious music, poetry, and the like to create a mood of reverence) of Pahnke's experiment was a kind of community in itself. The theoretical framework of the experience of many of the subjects reflected the heavy influence of Paul Tillich's theology. The subjects were well acquainted, apparently, with the theological categories of Tillich. The "threats" of non-being, meaninglessness, and condemnation were real to them. The search for true being, intense personal meaning, and freedom from condemnation pervaded their experience. The recovery or discovery of these gifts of spiritual reality were some of the fruits of their use of drugs. The context of the biblical understanding of the Holy Spirit both illuminates and corrects this set and setting. But the few cases reported verbatim by the subjects represent a sort of nature mysticism or, to use R. C. Zaehner's words, "an uprush from the collective unconscious."[15] This chides the biblicist with the extent to which the "secular man" is hungry for community and yet ignorant of the classical sources of the Christian faith. As the psychedelic experiences stand, they represent man's search for a community. However, the quest for community is addressed "to whom it may concern" at a "general delivery" window.

Furthermore, the "experiencers" of these drugs say they can better absorb the paradoxes of life and death. Nevertheless, their writings are as unaccepting as J. D. Salinger's in that they ignore the ambiguity in the necessity of role-taking, as well as its hazards. Many of Salinger's characters do reject the "phoniness" of conventional social roles. The Christ appears in the most unconventional of persons, such as an old fat lady. However, as Salinger's Holden Caulfield and his old fat lady are recognized and affirmed, even they must, if they continue to live among people at all, take their *part* in life. They are not the whole show. They take a role. This is what I mean by the ambiguity in the necessity as well as the hazards of role-taking. For example, the Apostle Paul relinquished his "role" as one "advanced beyond many of [his] own age" among the Jews. But in his later experience with the Christians he also assumed the role of the Apostle to the Gentiles. He did this only after the Holy Spirit guided the church at Antioch to set him and Barnabas apart for the work to which the Holy Spirit had called them (Acts 13:1–3). The resolution of this ambiguity is a fantasy. Roles obscure reality *and* symbolize reality. The idolatry of roles obscures reality. The aesthetic indecisiveness and uncommitment of the beatnik who rejects all roles *can* be a vital protest against this idolatry. At the same time, it *can* be a fearful freezing of the beatnik into the neurotic assumption that he or she is an exception from any kind of responsibility, especially work. Role-taking is *both* hazardous and necessary. To remove the hazard or the necessity seems to be a desire of the drug-takers which contradicts their profession of increased capacity to bear the paradoxes and ambiguities of life.

The second difference between the Christian experience of the Holy Spirit and the mystical experiences induced by psychedelic drugs is one of naturalness versus artificial experience. The Holy Spirit works through the normal processes of the mind—attention, data collection through the senses, remembering, associating, perceiving, dreaming.

We know that hypnosis and narcosynthesis are "instant entrances" into the wider depths of consciousness. Misuse and popular gamesmanship in the use of hypnosis for therapeutic purposes, however, did not cause Freud to abandon it as a tool. He did so because its results were too brief and "capricious." He turned to the use of a reclining position of relaxation, dream study, and free association. Even then he discovered that the character of his relationship of transference-affect was more important than his techniques, though this took longer to establish. S. I. Hayakawa speaks of the "set and setting" of our culture in which people are once again asking for shortcuts through the use of drugs:

We live in an advertising culture. Rolaids offer us instant relief from indigestion. Clairol offers us instant youth and beauty. The new Mustang makes Casanovas out of Casper Milquetoasts. Is it any wonder that there lurks in many of us a hope that a product can be found that offers instant relief from all spiritual ills—instant insight, instant satori?[16]

In answering his own rhetorical question, Hayakawa asks for a more *disciplined* and time-tested use of all our senses. He asks again: "Why disorient your beautiful senses with drugs and poisons before you have half discovered what they can do for you?"[17] This discipline, seen from the biblical perspective of the Holy Spirit, would, if accepted, followed, and sustained in practice, open the consciousness through the use of *all* the senses and not just the sense of hearing of words. It would include the observation of behavior, both internally and externally, the conception of broader overviews of events in their totality, and the search for the sources of energy in the Holy Spirit which sustain life and enhance daily growth. As the Apostle Paul puts it:

> . . . it is written,
> "What no eye has seen, nor ear heard,
> nor the heart of man conceived,
> what God has prepared for those who love him,"
> God has revealed to us through the Spirit. For the Spirit searches everything, even the depths of God (I Corinthians 2:9–10).

A third contrast between the Christian experience of the Holy Spirit and the drug-induced mystical experience is the time factor in the spiritual journey, pilgrimage, or "trip" which the two have in common. Christians experiencing the Holy Spirit tend to consider it a lifelong journey or pilgrimage. The drug-induced "trips" tend to telescope all eternity into the very "nowness" of a given moment. Then the experience lives in memory until another "trip" is induced. The *transiency* of the LSD experiences

> . . . refers to the temporary duration of mystical consciousness to contrast to the relative permanence of the level of

usual experience. The special and unusual forms of consciousness . . . remain for anywhere from a matter of seconds to a few hours, and then disappear, returning the experiencer to his usual state of everyday consciousness.[18]

Contrast this with the long, unremitting pilgrimage of the Apostle Paul *after* receiving the Holy Spirit. He resisted the Jews in Damascus with his proofs that Jesus was the Christ (Acts 9:22). He escaped their plots to kill him. He was rejected by the disciples at Jerusalem because they were all afraid of him and did not believe that he was a disciple. He apparently had his own long psychological moratorium and lying-fallow period in Arabia. Through the Holy Spirit he was accepted by the church at Antioch. He was guided by the Holy Spirit on his missionary journeys. He was sustained by the Holy Spirit when on trial for his life. He built his teachings concerning release from the bondage of the law upon the freedom that the Spirit gives from the letter and paradoxicality of the law. This is more than mysticism; it is continued participation in the Spiritual Presence that does away with the somewhat Manichaean distinction between spiritual illumination and the "usualness" of everyday experience. This in itself is a cleavage in the unity of life.

Not only the Apostle Paul, but later explorers also have been on spiritual journeys or "trips" into the self. Esther M. Harding, a Jungian psychoanalyst, has minutely analyzed John Bunyan's great allegory of the inner life, *Pilgrim's Progress.* She uses it to "mark out, as it were, a map of the journey of the soul."[19] She rejects easy shortcuts for the spiritual journey by saying that "there are no wide roads or easily found paths; the solution of one's difficulties is by means of stepping stones—individual steps taken one at a time—through or over the pits of uncertainty at the beginning of the quest."[20]

Bunyan's seventeenth-century originals in religious experience, however, have been compressed into fewer and fewer steps to salvation. Even in the 1850's Nathaniel Hawthorne satirized the commercialization of *Pilgrim's Progress* in his remarkable story of "The Celestial Railroad." The tourist, arriving at the City of Destruction, could go away again by paying a fare on the Celestial Railroad. All the difficult places in the road had been paved and smoothed; no discipline was required. The iron cage of despair, the battle with Appolyon, and all the rest were either used as displays for tourists or reenacted as if they were the real thing.[21] It was a sort of 1850 version of Knotts' Berry Farm combined with Disneyland! This kind of inauthenticity is the cultural atmosphere of both the LSD cults and the "cheap grace" evangelists of today. Pay your fare and take the trip. But both physicians and disciplined ministers point to the "capricious" results of LSD and "cheap grace" evangelism.

A fourth contrast between the Christian experience of the Holy Spirit and drug-induced mystical states is an ethical contrast. The drug-induced experiences reveal in bold relief the self-deceptions, the facades, the gamesmanship, and the inauthenticity of the lives of people who are constricted by roles. The psychedelic drugs expand and open the self to the vast potential it has lying unused. But once again the drugs do not define the limitations of human existence, the boundaries of human possibility. They tend to leave the subject with a childlike illusion of omnipotence. These feelings are best described in Kierkegaard's "aesthetic man," who wills all but chooses nothing. The necessities of ethical choice are alien to the aesthetic man. But the spiritual life in the Holy Spirit is experienced as a "long haul" and not a short "trip." The person is presented with ethical choices in the scope of his own personal development as well as the kairoi of history.

The Christian experience of the Holy Spirit, however, defines the nature of our relationship to God: We are creatures of his, his children (Romans 8:16). He is the source of moral expectations: love, joy, peace, good temper, kindness, goodness, fidelity, gentleness, self-control (Galatians 5:22). Love abides when all other gifts of the Holy Spirit fail (I Corinthians 13). God pours his Holy Spirit into the spirit of man, energizing him with ethical power (Romans 5:5). He has not given us a spirit of timidity, but one of power, love, and self-control (II Timothy 1:7).[22]

The very presence of LSD as an uncontrolled bio-chemical provides a social and ethical as well as a personal moral dilemma:

A review of the advantages of LSD as an incapacitating agent will help understanding of the interest of the military in this esoteric chemical. It can be cheaply and easily made. Its enormous potency would be an important factor in wartime use. A saboteur could carry enough in an overcoat pocket to produce serious, temporary effects on all the inhabitants of a megapolis if only he could distribute it equally. The contents of a two-suiter piece of luggage will hold an amount sufficient to disable every person in the United States. It is quite soluble in water and only slowly loses its activity in chlorinated water supplies. A short period of boiling does not destroy LSD in solution. Detection is extremely difficult because it is tasteless, odorless and colorless. The inhalation of particles suspended in the air is equally effective as a casualty producer. No doubt food upon which LSD spray has fallen will remain contaminated for days, although the substance could be removed by thorough washing with pure water. The intact skin will not be penetrated, but if some of the material is deposited on the fingers, their brief contact with the mouth may be sufficient to transmit an effective dose.

The city exposed to a successful LSD attack presumably will cease to function. The inhabitants will be so bemused with the odd things that are happening to them and their neighbors that for half a day an aggressor force could take over without substantial resistance. According to the news releases, by dawn of the next day everyone will be fit to work under the new management. Hopefully, the earlier, unsophisticated view has been abandoned by those concerned with strategic planning. It is not that simple.[23]

These effects are staggering, but they are less likely to happen than is the individual pushing of the drug on a black market basis.

The expansion of the consciousness is a psychological problem. The limit of its expansion is an ethical problem. Both call for a religious encounter of the spirit of man with the Spirit of God.

A fifth contrast between contemporary "God-talk" about the Holy Spirit and the controversy which rages around the use of psychedelic drugs is not unfavorable to the Holy Spirit but to our lack of experimental and empirical testing of our utterances about the Christian experience of the Holy Spirit. We tend to be inarticulate about these experiences, to consider them more intensely personal than our sex lives by far, or, at best, to speak of them in declarative moods that end discussion. As a result our audiences think of the witness to the Holy Spirit as being out of reach of experimental inquiry. The command to test the spirits to see whether they be of God is ignored.

Instead, we play what Eric Berne calls the game of "greenhouse." A person tells his experience as if to show us a beautiful orchid he has grown. And our *one* appropriate response is to exclaim: "Isn't it beautiful!" Grammatically this is a question. Empirically it is not. It is an exclamation.

I have known three persons in my life who took an empirical testing approach to their experience of the Holy Spirit, but only one of them was trained in the scientific method. Walter N. Johnson of North Carolina and J. Rufus Mosely of Georgia were the first two. Anton Boisen, the third, was the scientist. Boisen assumed that the important test of religious experience was "not between what is normal and what is pathological in religious experience, but between victory and defeat on the battlefield of the inner life." He sought by the case method to identify "authentic records of experiences comparable in severity" to those he had observed in psychotic patients, "but experiences in which the outcomes had unquestioned validity from the standpoint of the results attained."[24] Such records were not common, nor were their contents studied objectively and comprehensively. Yet Boisen dared to lay the contents of his own psychotic episodes on the printed page for men to study empirically. He himself recorded memories of his own hospitalization for mental disorder. In his book *Out of the Depths*[25] he records "the firsthand evidence" which was the basis for his authority as an explorer. The ideas he handles are certainly similar enough to those of Pahnke's experimenters to justify detailed comparison. Yet Boisen laid hold of the results of these experiences as a struggle of the soul over a lifetime of suffering and worship. He taught his students to find the sense in the nonsense of the psychotic person and to know that it often takes more than one generation to tell who is crazy. Such was a thirty-one-year-old psychotic man whom I interviewed in July, 1945, just days before the atom bomb was dropped on Japanese cities. The patient said:

> I existed before God existed and knew Adam and Eve when they were in the Garden. God said he was going to make man, and I knew it would get him into a lot of trouble, but I didn't try to stop him, because it was his business. As long as I can resist the atoms that come swirling like a black cloud from the planets the world will not come to an end. This is the twentieth century and time is running short.

Today the smog and Strontium 90 come swirling in upon us, and our major anxieties are about clean, unpolluted air and water. As I reflect on this young patient, I wonder why it was that he, and not the makers of atomic bombs, who had to have a prefrontal lobotomy to enable him to live more "normally" in a world like ours!

The Spirit of God is the *Spiritus Creator* and the *Spiritus Rector*—both creating life and keeping it at health. But our fear of each other and our need for the securities of affluent noise close us both to him and to ourselves. We need an experimental laboratory in which the religious genius of man in encounter with the Holy Spirit may be put to the test of observation and record. The chaotic and primeval expansions of the consciousness can be studied under laboratory conditions with socially disabled persons such as the psychotic patient just described. The expansion of the consciousness by psilocybin, mescaline, and LSD can be studied in such double-blind experiments as Pahnke conducted at Harvard.

More subtle and pedestrian, however, is the need for an empirical study of the "opening" of the consciousness through the natural, everyday means which either are not used at all or have become so routine as to be unnoticed or even rejected. Ours is an affluent society, bent on security through satisfaction and stimulation of the appetites and the senses. What kinds of revelations would come to a group of twenty persons, carefully selected as to such things as medical history, social and psychological health, clarity of purpose and meaning in life, who were led by the Holy Spirit together over a period of forty days and nights with no "roles" assigned, with a survival-level diet, with no access to telephone, radio, or television, with only manual labor to do, under a vow of verbal silence except for the written and read word? What kinds of reading would they want to take with them? What kinds of new things would come to their attention? What old and forgotten experiences would return to their memories? What kinds of daydreams would preoccupy them? What temptations would beset them? What would their sleep patterns be like? What kinds of night dreams could they record? What kinds of focus would their sense of the presence and leading of the Holy Spirit take? Then, having been led back into the ordinary world as we live it, what would be their evaluation of it, of themselves, and of their relationship to other people who had not had this tour of deprivation with the Holy Spirit? One can only venture a hunch that the major difference between this experiment and the psilocybin experiment would be its focus: Curiosity and quick results would tend to attract persons to a project using drugs and requiring only seventy-two hours. Commitment and decision would be required of persons volunteering for a forty-days-and-nights psychological moratorium on role-playing, satiation of appetites, and overstimulation of senses.

Another hunch is that this very kind of deprivation may account for much of the unusual spiritual perception of some persons placed in prison—like John Bunyan—forced into hiding from persecution—like Anne Frank —held in concentration camps—like Viktor Frankl—or deliberately renouncing the roles and affluences of life—like Albert Schweitzer. A laboratory situation aimed to produce such an appetite and sensory deprivation pattern would provide helpful clues for the clarification, corroboration, and correction of the conclusions about the use of drugs. The criteria of classical mystical experience (see Pahnke's statement on page 17) cannot be removed from the context of commitment to God and fellowship with the Holy Spirit. Discipline of appetite and senses provides the "set and setting" for the expansion of consciousness. The biblical witness concerning the Holy Spirit sets forth the covenant of belief in Jesus Christ and participation in the Holy Spirit. This covenant provides a "set" beyond that of a chapel and "cloud music."

(2)

Nonverbal Communication
and the Help of the Holy Spirit

Before the discovery of the New World, Mediterranean countries were prone to stamp a picture of the Pillars of Hercules on their coins, with the words underneath, *Ne plus ultra,* "There is nothing beyond." After the discovery of the New World, they removed the word *Ne* and their coins read instead, *Plus ultra,* "There is more beyond." Words in the human consciousness are like the Pillars of Hercules: they separate the small sea of human awareness from the uncharted regions beyond.

Contemporary psychology and psychotherapy have begun to describe the whole new world of nonverbal communication. There is "more beyond" the verbal constrictions of our wordy little worlds. Man's abilities to communicate nonverbally as well as his nonverbal activities can be correlated with the indwelling work of the Holy Spirit as we know him biblically and come to know him experientially. The writers of the Book of Acts, the Fourth Gospel, and the Epistle to the Romans attest to the continued activity of the Creator and Redeemer in the work of the Holy

Spirit after the historical encounter of man with the Word of God in the flesh of Jesus, the Christ. The gift of the Holy Spirit enabled men of different languages each to understand in his own language. The realm of subhuman nature participates with man in feelings that are "internal and unexpressed," in the birth of new life in the Spirit. Man himself is not alone in his struggles. The Holy Spirit supports our helplessness. "Left to ourselves we do not know how to word our prayers or how to offer them. But in those inarticulate groans which rise from the depths of our being, we recognize the voice of none other than the Holy Spirit."[1]

The nonverbal, inarticulate realm of the divine human encounter is often interpreted negatively as a weakness. The creative dimensions are missed. We lay such store by the verbal that inarticulateness is culturally stamped as "inferior" by a word-laden society. As Margaret Mead has said:

> The artist and the photographer are still not only paid less than the writer but those who are gifted in a thousand other ways are penalized, for if they do not have a "degree," they are debarred from one activity after another. . . . all the "degrees" are based on an ability to use words. People cannot graduate from anything today because they can paint a beautiful picture, restore a disturbed child to health, comfort the dying or design a new kind of computer.[2]

Admittedly, we are dealing with a paradox of the creative and destructive nature of both verbal and nonverbal experience, but the destructive possibilities of words and wordiness are often omitted from the paradox. Robert Cohen catches the tension of the polarity when he says:

> It is most impelling to observe how verbal language, which evolved as an instrument to describe, to define, to sing, to

acquaint man with the thought of another, which binds time and makes each man heir to the efforts of his brother (and a potential slave to the past) can destroy its maker. . . . This possibility arises from a lessened ability to recognize and hence respond to important fundamental sense impressions.[3]

The word is spoken from a distance and heard from a distance. Hearing is a "distance" sense. The senses of taste, smell, and touch are the "close" senses. Motion is seen with eye. Both the eye and the hand are nonverbal communicators and receptors. Overdependence upon words lessens their acuity.[4] As Alfred Korzybski has said, words cannot really express the objective nature of things as they are. There is a chasm of difference between things in themselves and the way we verbally describe them.

This difference, being *inexpressible* by words, cannot be expressed by words. We must have *other means* to indicate this difference. We must show with our hand, by pointing with our finger to the object, and by being silent outwardly as well as inwardly, which silence we may indicate by closing our lips with the other hand. . . . On this last level, we can look, handle, but *must* be silent.[5]

Albert Einstein recognized this when he said that words, written or spoken, did not seem to play any role in his mechanism of thought. "The psychical entities in my case are . . . visual and some of muscular type. Conventional words and other signs have to be sought for laboriously only in a secondary stage."[6] Amos N. Wilder, in speaking of the language of the gospel says that "Jesus himself spoke in short aphorisms and oracles and tightly knit parables, but also, we may say, in silences."[7]

From both the point of view of the Christian life in the Holy Spirit and that of a social psychology of nonverbal communication, several convergences of the religious and the scientific understanding of human experience can be focused.

"Playacting" and the Spirit of Truth

Shakespeare perceived the "playacting" character of human life when he said:

> All the world's a stage
> And all the men and women merely players;
> They have their exits and their entrances;
> And one man in his time plays many parts . . .
> *As You Like It,* Act II, Scene 7

Jacob Moreno identified three kinds of roles or "parts" which people "play":

. . . (a) the psychosomatic roles, such as the sleeper, the eater, the walker; (b) psychodramatic roles, as *a* mother, *a* teacher, *a* Negro, *a* Christian, etc.; and (c) social roles, *the* mother, *the* son, *the* daughter, *the* Christian. The genesis of roles goes through two stages, role perception and role enactment.[8]

A *person,* however, is more than, other than, and different from the "roles" he perceives and enacts. He longs with feelings that are unutterable to be cared for, for himself alone and not in one or another of the above-named roles. He hungers and thirsts for a genuinely human existence in which he can be and appear just as he is. Yet this prayer is only vaguely felt, difficult, if not impossible, to express, and even more to be understood when expressed. Moreno invented psychodrama as a spontaneous dropping of one's own role and taking on of that of another person. In a dramatic and intentional shift of roles, glimpses of the reality of oneself and the other person could be gained as a kind of seeing and feeling not captive to words. The tendency and the ability to empathize, the expansion of the variety of one's relationships to other people, and the definiteness with which one empathizes are all increased in such role-taking experiences.[9] These momentary releases from one's preoccupation with his own roles tends to free him for a time. He finds what he saw, heard, and felt difficult, if not impossible, to verbalize. For these reasons, the place of drama in the education of the minister should be enlarged. The nonverbal communication of the gospel through the "between-the-lines" messages of a play often provides understanding not possible in sermons. The use of silent pauses in music, for example, can say much. But this mode of communication is neglected in preaching.

The superficiality of personal relationships, with its distance, its distrust, and its deceptiveness, is maintained when one constantly relies on his "role" or "roles." In order to understand roles, we do not listen to what people say, we watch what they do. The words of persons tend to reflect the way their social roles have "programmed" their lives. At best, these roles are a *part* and not the whole of a person's self. They do not express either the depth or the totality of a person's being. Albert Camus has the lawyer in his soliloquy known as *The Fall* say:

At times people on their deathbeds seemed to me convinced of their roles. The lines spoken by my poor clients always struck me as fitting the same pattern. . . . I lived my whole life under a double code. . . . A ridiculous fear pursued me, in fact, one could die without having confessed all one's lies. Not to God or to one of his representatives. . . . No, it was a matter of confessing to men, to a friend, to a beloved woman, for example. Otherwise, were there but one lie hidden in a life, death made it definitive.[10]

The nature of life becomes a game unless the spirit of candor has its way. Sometimes the game is so harmless as to be ridiculous, sometimes so confusing as to be hurtful, sometimes so lethal as to destroy people. But the game is one of deception to avoid intimacy.

Such was the deceptiveness of Ananias and Sapphira as they lied to the Holy Spirit. But the opposite was true of the Apostle Paul when he said:

We have renounced disgraceful, underhanded ways; we refuse to practice cunning or to tamper with God's word, but by the open statement of the truth we would commend ourselves to every man's conscience in the sight of God. And even if our gospel is veiled, it is veiled only to those who are perishing. In their case the god of this world has blinded the minds of the unbelievers, to keep them from seeing the light of the gospel of the glory of Christ, who is the likeness of God. For what we preach is not ourselves, but Jesus Christ as Lord, with ourselves as your servants for Jesus' sake. For it is the God who said, "Let light shine out of darkness," who has shone in our hearts to give the light of the knowledge of the glory of God in the face of Christ (II Corinthians 4:2–6).

Robert Frost said it this way in his poem "Revelation":

> We make ourselves a place apart
>   Behind light words that tease and flout,
> But oh, the agitated heart
>   Till someone find us really out.
>
> 'Tis pity if the case require
>   (Or so we say) that in the end
> We speak the literal to inspire
>   The understanding of a friend.

45

But so with all, from babes that play
At hide-and-seek to God afar,
So all who hide too well away
Must speak and tell us where they are.[11]

Ways of Improving Nonverbal Communication

A reliable proving ground for our communication with each other at the nonverbal level would be the conscious practice of "experiencing the other side," the various roles those we regularly deal with—the other members of our families, the student body, the faculty, a deacon, a housewife—have to fulfill.When we do this, we catch basically ineffable apprehensions of the silent level of each other's being. We may have only a sentence with which to capture our venom as did Marc Conley's character in *Green Pastures* who, seeing the crucifixion, said, "I guess being God ain't no bed of roses."

A further excitement to human growth is to search out ways to *do* things nonverbally that are not ordinarily expected of us in our roles. You will notice I said *do* things, not *say* things. For example, Jesus said that David and his men, when they were hungry, went into the Temple and ate the bread from the altar in the days of Abiathar the priest. Jesus said this after he and his men had gathered and eaten grain on the Sabbath. His was a ministry of the unexpected because his acts were guided by the spontaneity of the Spirit and not by prepackaged role expectations. Here they did the unexpected in their psychosomatic role as "eaters" (they *were* hungry as total persons, even though it was the Sabbath).

Similar unexpected shifts of role—the father who asks his son's advice, the professor who makes a pastoral call, the pastor who remembers little children's names, the minister who refuses a ministerial discount—are *seen* and *felt*. Thus a degree of authenticity and renunciation of verbal phoniness is achieved.

The Holy Spirit in the New Testament is referred to as the Spirit of truth who "will guide you into all the truth" (John 16:13). The Christian receives the word of truth in Christ, and this is "sealed with the promised Holy Spirit" (Ephesians 1:13). The gift of the Word of God in Christ is itself inexpressible. "Thanks be to God for his inexpressible gift" (II Corinthians 9:15)! Persons encountered by the Spirit of truth were speechless, as was Zechariah. When he came out of the Temple, "he could not speak to them . . . he made signs to them and remained dumb" (Luke 1:22). Similarly, the Apostle Paul was blinded by the encounter with the Christ (Acts 9:8), and his eyes were opened upon receiving the Holy Spirit (Acts 9:18).

To the contrary, deception comes, not from the Holy Spirit, but from Satan. Satan "fills the heart to lie." In the Johannine Gospel, the Devil is referred to as "a liar and the father of lies" (John 8:44). In the Johannine letters, the word of truth is measured by the Christ, and the antichrist is equated with a lie (I John 2:22). Confession of Jesus as the Christ is the gateway to the knowledge of the Spirit of God and the criterion for "test[ing] the spirits to see whether they are of God" (I John 4:1–2). If the late dating of these documents implies an incursion of Hellenistic mythology, then Second Thessalonians identifies the activity of Satan with pretense, deception, delusion, and the desire to believe what is false (II Thessalonians 2:9–12).

We must disengage ourselves from the prescientific

ontology of the Greco-Roman world. However, even when we have done so, we still have the strong ethical imperative that men who would know God and each other in depth must renounce the facework of role deception. They must move beyond the power that words, names, titles, and roles have to menace and distort the authentic work of the Spirit of truth. Not by chance do the Quakers simultaneously emphasize the power of silence, the centrality of the Holy Spirit, and the potential destruction of a community by the deceptiveness of roles, positions, titles, and "the noise of solemn assembly." Their contribution to our life together in God needs to be rediscovered and reaffirmed.

Repression and Religious Inarticulateness

A second focus for correlating the realities of nonverbal communication with the work of the Holy Spirit is through a reappraisal of the meaning of repression for mid-twentieth century religious experience. Repression "may be briefly defined as the active process of keeping out and ejecting, banishing from consciousness, the ideas or impulses that are unacceptable to it."[12] Freud defined *primal repression* as "a denial of entry into consciousness" of any mental or ideational presentation of an impulse. Thus the feeling or impulse remains nonverbal; its content never takes the shape of symbol or sign. Freud conceived of the impulses of hostility and tender eroticism as being most often repressed. He lived and worked in a Victorian era of much "God-talk," great silence about sexuality, hostility, and attendant ideas and impulses. The mass media were either in their infancy or nonexistent. His patients' eyes and ears were not satiated by the advertising industry's verbalism about sex and power. The repression of these impulses was successful, and they remained in the inarticulate or at least the inchoate in their expression in consciousness.

However, the tides of circumstance and our cultural milieu have produced a very different kind of repressed material today. That which is excluded from consciousness, especially in the religious home of today, is not sex—thanks to mass media. Rather, it is the articulation of distinctly religious feelings, aspirations, and ideas. These remain inarticulate ordinarily and poorly formed at best. The church lost out, says David C. McClelland, "because it became insensitive to the revelations of God and stuck stubbornly to former revelations, ideas, and images which have lost much of their meaning for thinking people."[13] He said further that undergraduate counselors and patients "talk readily enough about their sex lives, but unwillingly and with great hesitation about their religious convictions. . . . It is not sex which is a delicate subject in our generation but religion."[14] McClelland speaks of this as a "taboo against religion" and refers to the *"unconscious* religious assumptions of psychoanalysis." For this unconsciousness to be effective, *repression* must be at work.

Yet, as true as this observation is, it is only a part of the truth. Religious experience calls for articulation and sharing with others. It is also a kind of experience that by its very nature both imposes and endorses silence. The deepest kinds of religious concern have a native shyness about words and wordiness. The seemingly urbane, "secular," cosmopolitan Dag Hammarskjöld would not have used the interior simplicities of his *Markings* as social chitchat at a party. Nor would these necessarily have been "repressed." They simply would be no one's business and too important to him personally to be bandied about as topics for light conversation. This disclaimer must be entered to balance out the excellent interpretation of McClelland about the repression of religious experience. Even so, other analysts of personality—such as Harry Stack Sullivan—illuminate both the repression of religious feelings and the endorsement of silence about them.

Sullivan further sharpens our understanding of how our consciousness constricts itself in order to exclude the painful, the unacceptable. He speaks of "selective inattention." We do not like to discover the unobtainable. We are powerless, regardless of all cooperation of those about us. We treat such unobtainable objects *as if* they did not exist. We inadvertently "inattend," i.e., fail to become aware of, that which reminds us of our helplessness by its unobtainableness. God is a reminder both of our helplessness and of his own unobtainableness. Functioning *as if* God does not exist removes us from the necessity of confessing our weaknesses and limitations.

"God-Talk" and the Holy Spirit

This does not satisfy the linguistic analysts who insist upon more logical and empirically significant language in theological "God-talk." William T. Blackstone of the University of Georgia asks for "metatheological" analyses which have the "greatest explanatory power" and which "best account for the logical behavior of religious statements."[15]

Yet Erich Fromm speaks of the "repressedness" of such insistence upon logical limitations of awareness. He calls language, logic, and content a "social filter." "To the degree to which I can rid myself of this filter and can experience myself as the universal man, that is, to the degree which repressedness diminishes, I am in touch with the deepest sources within myself, and that means all of humanity."[16] Fromm asserts that the repressed man "instead of experiencing things and persons . . . is only in touch with words."[17]

Neither the linguistic analysis of Blackstone nor the mystical humanism of Fromm would be compatible with a frank statement of the Christian experience of the Holy Spirit. The repressive effects of logical positivism make the mention of the Holy Spirit another form of "God-talk." Even the use of such language would be challenged by the logical positivist. Steadfast insistence upon the power of the Holy Spirit to relax our repressions and put us in touch not only with our own unconscious but with the whole creation also would have a heuristic effect on both the linguistic analyst and the Christian. The Christian commitment to participation in the Holy Spirit frets and aggravates the logician. It calls out emotions in him of which he is unaware and reminds him of his own religious strivings. On the other hand, the challenge of the linguistic analyst calls the Christian to experimental verification of his relationship to the Holy Spirit. It prompts him to ask: Is belief in the Holy Spirit simply a logical proposition for me, or have I experimentally validated his presence in my life? Have I consensually validated my experience with other Christians? Do we have a fellowship based on that which we have together experienced of the Holy Spirit? Even though we do not have words, can we "point" to things that we have seen happen by reason of our participation in the Holy Spirit?

The Namelessness of the Holy Spirit

On the other hand, the mystical humanism of Erich Fromm is willing to get along with no name for the "unrepressed life." The theistic connotations of the Person of the Holy Spirit are themselves verbal idolatries to Fromm. Yet the Christian asks: Does the personal focusing of the mystical consciousness in the Holy Spirit in terms of the Giver of Life in God and the Redeemer of Life in Jesus Christ provide meaning and context of personal relationship not available in Zen Buddhism? Can an ethical *esprit de corps* of a fellowship of believers in Christ become possible in a responsible I–Thou encounter not available in a purely individualistic mysticism? The burden of proof for this rests upon the Christian community itself in terms of the "fruits of the Spirit" of which Paul speaks. Even the Christian concern with the Holy Spirit has been a divisive factor among some Christians since the time of the Corinthian correspondence. The Johannine literature asks for the "testing of the spirits" to see whether they are of God. Participation in the Holy Spirit as a way of life today may be viewed with a credibility gap so wide that modern man often finds it bordering upon the unreal. If this is so, simple assertions on my part do not bridge that gap. Some sort of face-to-face conversation alone can do that adequately.

Caution in Nonverbal Communication

A word of caution can be learned from what is known about repressed concerns of persons. These cannot be brought to consciousness and commitment by direct means—exhortation, instruction, and frontal attack. These verbal attacks simply narrow the consciousness and increase ·the defenses. The repressed religious concerns must be elicited through the nonverbal "language of relationships": identification with a genuinely religious person who can be trusted, a counseling relationship aimed at the relaxation of defenses, the exploration of what might be called "the secular man's ultimate concerns," and the clarification of the meaning of grace, forgiveness, and lasting hope through nonverbal expressions of acceptance, understanding, and personal commitment on the part of the pastoral counselor.

The pastoral counselor of the last half of this century will be called upon to "make conscious" the repressed material of the religiously inarticulate. One cannot *speak* of these materials because they *are* nonverbal. But he can point to them, and he that has eyes can see them. In this both he and his counselee are *enabled* by the Holy Spirit.

But the point of common concern among Christian, Zen Buddhist, and linguistic analyst alike is that of the source of man's freedom from the "tyranny of words." From this oppression all three join in an unutterable prayer for freedom. The *repression,* which is itself a word for "bondage," is the common enemy.

Nonverbal Communication and Personal Growth in the Spirit

The developmental angle of vision is a third perspective from which to perceive the work of the Holy Spirit and the role of nonverbal communication in a social psychology. What role does nonverbal communication play in the growth and development of the person in society?

Infancy and Preverbal Communication

Jurgen Ruesch and Weldon Kees say that the infant, especially in the first year of his life, "literally 'speaks' with his whole body." The primary purpose of the nonverbal "bodily" language of an infant is to get help. Nonverbal language of sign, action, and object communication is primarily a signaling for help. The semaphore of an infant—who has no language but a cry, a grunt, a groan, a feverishly waved arm or kicked leg—is a cry for help out of helplessness.[18]

Adolescence and Nonverbal Communication

As the child matures into adolescence, the system of communication becomes more verbal. However, the appeals for help in a disturbed and unhappy adolescent may come in the form of behavior—often "bad" behavior. Verbal means of being "heard" or "attended to" by a parent, teacher, and pastor break down. "Acting-out" behavior becomes the way of being heard. The community feeling of the adolescent subculture often takes the form of special ingroup language designed for intimacy within the group and exclusion of "outsiders," especially adults. The adult who mimics this language "breaks the code" of the secretiveness of teen-agers, who through language of their own create a private world of their own. The adult communicates much more effectively with adolescents when he respects this language as "theirs" and not "his." When he does this, a nonverbal "understanding" can develop by which, when the teen-ager is with the adult, he is treated *as an adult* insofar as is humanly possible. Language is one way of symbolizing this treatment.

Not only do adolescents develop their own ingroup language. They also tend to express their affection for adults in nonverbal ways. Their messages of affection get back to the parent through other people, not directly. A surprise visit of a college student to his mother on

Mother's Day with no sentimental words expressed *does* what he feels. Hence, the wise parent learns to *watch* what the adolescent *does* rather than be dismayed by what he says or does not say.

Adulthood and Nonverbal Communication

Among middle and upper class adults, bodily movement and meaningless sounds—groans, wails, grunts, and exclamations—in religious worship are "taboo." Nonverbal expressions must be highly ordered, as in the Lord's Supper or baptism, the use of the hymnbook or the Bible, or kneeling. The spontaneous expression of silent groans, tears, or nonsocialized exclamations is "out of bounds" in most "polite," "mature" Protestant worship.

Yet, the deepest appeals for help from worshipers ordinarily go unheard. For example, do we notice a person who remains seated after the service and does not chatter away in social magpie fashion, a person who wipes his or her face and moves quickly out before the benediction is over, a person who lags behind alone after most of the crowd is gone, a person who sits morosely and "washes" his face with his dry hands during the service?

"Speaking in Tongues" and Nonverbal Communication

It has been among the "well-to-do," the sophisticated, and superficially verbal that recent expressions of glossolalia have broken out. This recurring form of nonverbal communication was spoken of by the Apostle Paul as a childlike form of encounter with the Holy Spirit without understanding. This "preverbal" kind of religious experience seems to be a breakthrough of the deepest appeals for help in a person. As an infant crying without language, the glossolalic seeks to be heard by God and his neighbor. As Eduard Schweizer says, "The Holy Spirit never closes our heart. He tears it open continually for the sake of others, for the sake of community."[19] The experience of the Holy Spirit opens the consciousness, releases repressions, and communicates underlying unsolved problems. Many of these are serious, unresolved tensions. As one person put it,

Once I stopped seeking an experience, and desired only more of God, this awe-full "Baptism" came to me as I was praising God. I felt literally gripped by Someone. A great joy flooded into me and despite my inhibitions out of my mouth came perhaps fifteen minutes of ecstatic utterance, which was like background music to my marvelling and praising God within. After it ended, I felt renewed. I experienced a new freedom recognizable by those close to me.

Such an experience cannot be evaluated on a normal–abnormal continuum. Rather, it must be seen developmentally in terms of the work of the Holy Spirit in bringing into birth through groaning and travail a new being-in-relation of the whole person—not just his cognitive and verbal understanding—with God. It must be understood as the release of repressions. The rejected, "infantile" helplessness comes from our unconscious into consciousness. The birth of a new life does not mean full-grownness, however. The speech of the glossolalic is not matured, but it has the advantage of childlikeness. Jean Piaget, the outstanding expert on the language of the child, helps us here. He classifies language into two groups —egocentric and socialized. Egocentric language is characterized by (1) *repetition* of pleasant sounds for the pleasure they bring to the child's own ears; (2) *mono-logue,* wherein the child "talks to himself as though he were thinking aloud" (this is a soliloquy); (3) *dual or collective monologue,* in which outsiders are present but are not "expected to attend nor to understand."[20] Socialized speech is distinguished by the characteristics of criticism; commands, requests, and threats; questions; answers.

Piaget's description of the early speech of a child is precisely Paul's description of speaking in tongues. The breakthrough of a private, personal, unsocialized speech is the first fruit of spiritual consciousness as a person moves out of the completely inarticulate, or nonverbal.

Sullivan describes the consciousness that goes before the personally meaningful babbling as the "prototaxic," or preverbal, mode of experience. This is "the simplest, the earliest, and possibly the most abundant mode of experience." We are capable of experiencing this from the beginning of life. "The prototaxic mode is a very early form of . . . living as a living being."[21]

Reverie and the Holy Spirit

Experience-prior-to-language gets as close as we are capable of getting to those *reverie processes* which prepare us to express something, or to have something to say. As Sullivan says:

Reverie continues to be relatively untroubled by grammatical rules, the necessity for making complete sentences, and so on.

Incidentally, there are people who seem completely staggered when one talks about . . . wordless thinking; these people seem to have no ability to grasp the idea that a great deal of covert living . . . can go on without the use of words. The brute fact is, as I see it, that most of living goes on that way.[22]

Such wordless thinking and "living as a living being" in preparation for communication and speaking is the essence of both childlikeness and worship. Without such reverie, there is no vision and where there is no vision, the people perish. As William Wordsworth said:

> There are in our existence spots of time
> That with distinct pre-eminence retain
> A renovating virtue . . . our minds
> Are nourished and invisibly repaired.
> *The Prelude*, XII, 208

The Holy Spirit works through this reverie of wordless thinking and "living as a living being" as God's response to our helplessness. He makes intercession for us in our muted feelings. As Erich Fromm says, "we have to become children again, to experience the unalienated, creative grasp of the world; but in becoming children again, we are at the same time not children but fully developed adults."[23] Such childlikeness accepts helplessness without loss of face or dignity. We participate in the love of God shed abroad in our hearts through the Holy Spirit. We live as a living being in a galaxied universe in which "there is no speech, nor are there words; their voice is not heard; yet their voice goes out through all the earth, and their words to the end of the world" (Psalm 19:3–4).

I sat with a preadolescent child who was in the depths of grief. Neither she nor I could talk much. Yet we seemed to understand each other. She asked if I were in a hurry. I said No; as we both watched it rain outside. She asked why I was not in a hurry. I said that rarely did I find opportunity to be in the presence of a little girl who was not herself in a hurry. We sat in reverie and watched the sun come through the rain clouds. Then in sparkling array a rainbow appeared on the horizon. It made no noise as it appeared, and no words cluttered our knowledge of grief, beauty, friendship, and freedom from hurry and fear. Little did I know or have any intimation by such knowledge then that I was speechless. I was worshiping God through the Holy Spirit, and I was being prepared to say the last words of this chapter! But I was! Glory be to the Father, Son, and Holy Spirit!

(3)

The Holy Spirit and the
Ministry of Articulation

The previous chapter pointed to nonverbal communication and the intercession of the Holy Spirit at the level of the "unutterable." Yet it leaves us with the burden and calling of articulating—putting into words—the deepest concerns of our total beings, of being understood by and understanding each other. This understanding must be something more than definition, legal statement, and written agreements. These are exceptionally necessary when covenants collapse between us and when we substitute cleverness, deception, and hope of gain for open-hearted participation with each other in the gladness and singleness of heart generated by the Spirit of God.

Definition, legal statement, and written memoranda are necessary and useful in a bureaucratic milieu. In a political and ecclesiastical milieu such as we live in today, diplomacy is a way of life. It is not all evil. We can learn much from effective sciences of diplomacy. But when we put into words our deepest concerns in order to be understood by and to understand each other as total persons, much more is needed than definition, legal statements, and written agreements. Genuine understanding is the kind of articulation needed here. As Emmanuel Cellar, U.S. Congressman from Brooklyn, said to one of his opponents: "We can give you the answers, but we cannot give you the understanding."[1] This important distinction accepts basic problems of the way words both convey and conceal understanding. The German language distinguishes between "answers" and "understanding" as different kinds of articulation: *Erklären* means "to explain, account for, clear up, declare, pronounce, interpret, define." In the law it is used to refer to a deposition or a manifesto. A variation of it—*Erklärungsschrift*—is used to mean "commentary." But the kind of articulation we are thinking of here is referred to as *verstehen*—"to understand, grasp, know well." Variations of it mean "to know what's what; to know on which side your bread is buttered; to understand another; to come to an agreement with; to be skilled and disciplined as an expert in a matter; to come to an understanding of another."

The distinction between articulation as definition and pronouncement, on the one hand, and articulation as understanding and action based on insight, on the other, provides a ground of interaction between our knowledge of God through the Holy Spirit, our ministry of counseling as pastors, and the art and science of psychotherapy. The exploration of this ground of common concern is the substance of this chapter.

The most difficult point is the best place to start. In Mark 13:11 we find these words:

And when they bring you to trial and deliver you up, do not be anxious beforehand what you are to say; but say whatever is given you in that hour, for it is not you who speak, but the Holy Spirit.

In Luke 12:11–12 is a similar verse:

And when they bring you before the synagogues and the rulers and the authorities, do not be anxious how or what you are to answer or what you are to say; for the Holy Spirit will teach you in that very hour what you ought to say.

In Matthew 10:19–20 the basic material is expressed somewhat differently in what was probably a different context:

When they deliver you up, do not be anxious how you are to speak or what you are to say; for what you are to say will be given to you in that hour; for it is not you who speaks, but the Spirit of your Father speaking through you.

In Luke 21:12–15 no reference is made to the Holy Spirit or the Spirit of the Father; only a direct promise of Jesus himself is made:

. . . they will lay their hands on you and persecute you, delivering you up to the synagogues and prisons, and you will be brought before kings and governors for my name's sake. This will be a time for you to bear testimony. Settle it therefore in your minds, not to meditate beforehand how to answer; for I will give you a mouth and wisdom, which none of your adversaries will be able to withstand or contradict.

In the Fourth Gospel (John 14:25–27) is a similar passage with no reference to persecution or courtroom trial. Yet all the same ingredients of promise, spontaneity, and basic security-in-trust are present:

These things I have spoken to you, while I am still with you. But the Counselor, the Holy Spirit, whom the Father will send in my name, he will teach you all things and bring to your remembrance all that I have said to you. Peace I leave with you; my peace I give to you; not as the world gives, do I give to you. Let not your hearts be troubled, neither let them be afraid.

Four basic identities are constant in all these references to the Holy Spirit and the ministry of articulation. These common themes give clues as to the meaning of the passages in *any* context, without doing violence to the changing contexts in which the four texts were written. In fact, these continuities of meaning of the texts also under-score the eschatological atmosphere of life-and-death struggle which surrounds especially the three Synoptic references as well as the more leisurely atmosphere of the Johannine account. The four basic identities which hold the texts in communion are as follows: (1) the realistic references to memory and its role in interaction with the Holy Spirit; (2) disciplined naïveté is a necessary pre-condition of the Holy Spirit's enlivening of the utterance of even the most informed persons; (3) a settled or "resolved" mind and the kinds of courage of conviction this requires for resolute action and clarity of thought; (4) a mood of openness and receptivity to all the gifts of God, especially the gift of the Holy Spirit and an expanded awareness in time of stress.

Memory and Interaction With the Holy Spirit

The memory is one of the lawful mental processes through which we interact with the Holy Spirit. Stephen was brought before the rulers and the authorities. He spoke his witness. He did not use a prepared script memorized by rote ahead of time with sweaty anxiety. But he did rehearse the whole history of the Jewish people from the appearance of the God of glory to Abraham. He underscored the Jewish pattern of killing prophets. He accused them of the murder of Jesus and the violation of the Law of Moses. As he began his speech, even those who sat at the council "saw that his face was like the face of an angel" (Acts 6:15). As he completed it, "he, full of the Holy Spirit," said that he saw "the Son of man standing at the right hand of God" (Acts 7:55–56). As they killed him, he asked that the Lord Jesus would receive his spirit and not hold their sins against them.

Stephen had a memory steeped in the knowledge and understanding of his people, the Jews. A sense of history was woven into the fabric of his being. The fresh memory of the words of Jesus on the cross were vivid either in his mind or in that of the reporter of the events of his death. To think of this as a "prepared" sermon is a sacrilege. Any speech he could have prepared would not have been appropriate. This was no lecture on history nor a commentary on the words of Jesus on the cross. This was the acetylene brilliance of a man on trial for his life, filled with the *pneuma* of God. For him the *eschaton* was at hand.

Dietrich Bonhoeffer, in a discussion with his students about preaching, said:

A sermon is relevant only when God is there. He is the one who makes its message concrete. . . . The preacher has no word of wisdom suited specially to the moment. He has to proclaim what he knows of God in the situation. The concrete situation represents only the material to which the word of God can be spoken. . . . The truly concrete situation is . . . the sinner standing before God and the answer to that situation is in the crucified and risen Lord.[2]

The enlivening of the memory by the Holy Spirit is in terms of the event of God in Jesus Christ. This gives a new perspective of long-accustomed facts. Suddenly that which one has known all along is catalyzed into a dramatic new organization with a meaning and an understanding not yet seen by the eye, heard by the ear, or grasped by the understanding. The *erklären* of already known data becomes a new creation of a vital *verstehen*. This kind of memory does not struggle at retention; it is overcome by unforgettableness.

In pastoral counseling, the task of the distinctly pastoral counselor is not the pronouncement and declaration of facts, truths, or even major doctrinal statements to the person who is seeking help or whom one is trying to assist. The deadly games people are playing with each other call for much more crucial care than this. As Eric Berne has said in his book *Games People Play*, the deadly games end up in the courtroom, the surgery, or the morgue. These situations are fraught with the possibility of divorce, attempted suicide, or murder. They are cramped with necessity for decision. The consciousness of those playing these deadly games is constricted to the immediate *now*. They want the pastor to "give them *the* answer" now. Invariably the counselee either has *no* sense of his own religious heritage, or sees no linkage between his way of life and the indwelling presence of God, or finds that the forms and facts of religion are not sufficiently alive in his life to enable him to understand the full sweep of his life in an hour of time. The counselor could easily give him "the answer," but he cannot give him the understanding. In the gathering of the two or three together in these crucial human situations, the person actualizes himself only when he *has* to do so. He must come to total despair before the *shekina* of the Lord can mean anything to him. Then "all that he has ever done" comes back to him in a new light, as it did for the woman at the well.

In the course of casework and psychotherapeutic endeavors to help persons in distress, the history-taking method is still an imperative necessity. This mobilization of the memory of the person and his family to relate his spiritual history is a necessary part of therapy. But it is a cold, unimaginative, and uninspired therapist who "takes a history" out of the person as if it were an inflamed appendix. The novice who assumes that "getting-all-the-facts" in a "dragnet" detective manner genuinely effects dynamic change in persons or enables him to understand them better is naïve indeed.

Ethical decisions are made in three different ways. In the realm of habit-formation, rules, codes, and rabbinical laws are the least common denominators of community decision. In the realm of prudential judgment, situational ethics tend to ameliorate the tension between day-to-day circumstances and the accumulated wisdom of the laws of God and man. However, the existential approach to ethical decision calls for vital, personal encounter with the Holy Spirit in the intensity of a life-and-death event in which no preparation is possible and for which no "rule" has been devised. How do these blend into each other?

In ethical decisions the rabbinical casuistic method abstracts the decision from the present living situation and settles matters on the basis of precedent. This is illustrated in the case of the evangelist who believes that God is a compendium of logically consistent propositions and goes to the would-be convert armed with his memorized texts and propositions. Such evangelism has been caricatured in James Michener's *Hawaii*. The "givenness" of a witness "in the hour" from the self-emptying of the missionary is missed by both Michener and his central character. The "on-the-spotness" of extemporaneous pastoral counseling, psychotherapy, ethical decision-making, and evangelism does not set aside the memory, however. The cruciality of the life situation and the previous discipline of the total person in the data of human experience and the raw materials of history make the difference in the kind of *material* with which the Holy Spirit has to work. The eschatological necessity of the Synoptic Gospels reveals an urgency that made a witness like that of Stephen's— though unrehearsed—a glowing array of lucid memories. The more placid apologetics of the Fourth Gospel, nevertheless, portray the Holy Spirit as working through the memory of the Christian disciple. Past disciplines in the teaching of Jesus are activated by the Holy Spirit at the time of the disciple's crucial testing. The Holy Spirit performs the ministry of articulation through the inspired memories of the acts of Jesus—as in Stephen's case—and the teachings of Jesus—as in the case of the writer(s) of the Fourth Gospel.

Disciplined Naïveté and the Holy Spirit

Disciplined naïveté is a necessary condition of the effective work of the Holy Spirit in even the most informed mind and memory. The preconceptions, presuppositions, biases, beloved hypotheses, and managed perfections of the legalist, the moralist, or the exhorter are "bracketed in." They are kept in abeyance. This "bracketing in" is a "disconnection" of previous memories, value judgments and decisions *in order* that the pure reality of the moment may be perceived to the fullest. Edmund Husserl expresses this in his discussion of the general structure of pure consciousness.

The bracketed matter is not wiped off the phenomenological slate, but only bracketed, and thereby provided with a sign that indicates the bracketing. Taking its sign with it, the bracketed matter is reintegrated in the main theme of the inquiry.[3]

This is more easily said than done: to put all my value system in brackets as I move into a crucial situation. This takes discipline. I must become as a little child before the pure facts, inasmuch as in me lies. Each crucial situation must lay aside as much of my *before*hand *pre*suppositions as possible. In Socratic language, I must be willing to know nothing in order genuinely to be wise. In Jesus' language, I must turn and become as a little child—open, awe-filled, naïve in the classical, not popular, sense of the word. This "disciplined naïveté" is an ingenuousness, an artlessness, an unaffected simplicity. As Helmut Thielicke says, "this is a kind of antithesis of theoretical reflection on ethics, [and] the moment of action confers a certain simplification."[4]

Such was the manner of Jesus when he was brought before the rulers and authorities. When the governor asked him, "Are you the King of the Jews?" Jesus said to him, "You have said so." He made no answer to the chief priests and elders. He gave Pilate "no answer, not even to a single charge" (Matthew 27:11–14). Whatever assumptions were expressed were theirs, not his. In the preparation for this hour he had disciplined himself in solitary prayer. He "bracketed in" the whole matter of his life. The course of Christian history is the story of how what

he did *not* say then has been and is still being "reintegrated into the main theme" of our encounter with ourselves and God.

The idea of disciplined naïveté at first glance seems
strange to the Holy Spirit's ministry of articulation. But
closer scrutiny brings a glow of recognition. For example,
as evangelists, we are hard pressed when called upon to
minister to an avowed atheist. We sit before his judgment
seat for being a Christian. We can go to him with carefully
prepared arguments, cleanly packaged proofs of God, and
the hardened bread of our memorized texts. As we do so
we are filled with anxiety along with prepared speeches.
We would do better to bracket in our own beliefs and
biases and move on the assumption of the Living Presence
of the Holy Spirit only. The main discipline is prayer that
we might *understand* this person in his totality, to perceive
the world from within him as he perceives it. The revelation that comes to us when we permit him to be the self
that he is, is a gift of the Spirit. The most carefully
prepared apology can be easily "withstood and contra-
dicted." A disciplined defenselessness and an inspired
understanding of the individual cannot. Whether he likes it
or not the "good news" of God comes to him in such an
encounter of openness and teachableness on our part.

Furthermore, in pastoral counseling, we "bracket in"
our own personal values when dealing with moral
offenders. Our values are not best communicated through
exhortation anyway. Rather, we move at the grossest of
offenses *as if* the whole matter were plain facts—no more,
no less. This does not mean that we have erased our
ethical values, even though we may be accused of doing
so. We have bracketed them in. In the testing situation we
rely upon the internal maturation of conscience in the
offender by the Holy Spirit. Our own values are later

reintegrated "when the person is able to receive them." We approach such situations, which involve crucial possibilities of court procedure, illness, or death, *with no* preconceived attack. The shutters of our awareness are opened their widest. The prayer for sensitivity to the whole range of possibilities frees us from the prison of *one* alternative in meeting these massive problems head-on. Instead, we are enabled by the power of the Spirit to see *other* and additional approaches to the powers of good and evil. The Holy Spirit is the Spirit of Innovation and Creativity, producing imaginative approaches to crucial individual and family counseling problems.

In turn, the counselee tends to experience this disciplined naïveté of the minister as understanding and forgiveness. If he is tempted to interpret this naïveté as stupidity (which is popularly meant by *naïveté*), then the expanded awareness of the minister quickly senses this. The Holy Spirit is the best teacher about the spirit of deception, fear, and contempt. The minister who practices "undisciplined naïveté" has "renounced disgraceful, underhanded ways . . . but by the open statement of the truth [commends himself] to every man's conscience in the sight of God" (II Corinthians 4:2). If he meets a person without a conscience or with a seared conscience, then participation in the Holy Spirit enables him to be among the first to know it.

This open declaration of one's self to persons runs cross-grained against prevalent misconceptions of psychology as a prepared "bag of tricks" to use to manipulate people. It contradicts the "labeling craze," whereby we feel that we have solved a problem if we can give the condition a name—either psychological or theological. For example, where are we other than where we began when we brand a person as a "sociopath" or as one of those "not elect unto salvation"? We are anxious, tense, fretful, and unsettled in our minds. That is where we are!

Freedom From Anticipatory Anxiety

The imperative command of Luke 21:14 has a military ring to it: "Settle it therefore in your minds, not to meditate beforehand how to answer." One figure of speech to clarify the command is the military command "At ease." The arms of the soldier obeying this command are in a relaxed condition, but ready for action. Another figure of speech pictures one settling his mind as a clear act of surrender. The anticipatory anxiety of "how to answer" is to be resolved by the act of surrender. Harry M. Tiebout uses this concept to interpret the beginning of recovery for the alcohol addict. He cannot begin to recover until he comes to despair and admits his helplessness. We who are addicted to "always having the answer" go into a panic at the thought of not having our "bottled answers" to hit when in stress. The act of surrender to God is no less a necessity for us than for the alcoholic.

Gabriel Marcel captures this in imagery well known to the student taking examinations:

A simple expression borrowed from everyday language is a help here: *to take one's time*. He who stiffens and rebels does not know how to take his time. . . . Take your time, an examiner would say to a flurried candidate. That means, do not force the personal rhythm, the proper cadence of your reflection, or even of your memory, for if you do you will spoil your chances. . . .[5]

The ministry of the Holy Spirit in the demonstrable processes of one's being moves just this way of "taking one's time." Furthermore, Viktor Frankl's conception of paradoxical intention as a sort of principle of reverse effect is another empirical description of the "settled" mind. *Excessive* effort in one direction—to succeed, to say the right thing, to have the right answer—often produces just the opposite result. Shakespearean wisdom would say that "in fearing to be spilt, we are spilt all over." In Franklin Roosevelt's words, "The only thing we have to fear is fear itself." In desiring too much to succeed, we fail; to say the right thing, we say the wrong thing; to have the right answer, we have the wrong one. The spiritual exercise of paradoxical intention is to desire *not* to succeed, *not* to say the right thing, *not* to have the right answer. Thus we exist freely and can be creative in the moment of testing.

The ability to do this! Ah! There is the rub! This is the reply of the unsettled, tense person. The affirmation of the New Testament is that the Holy Spirit is the Enabler, the Counselor, the Teacher who releases within us the power to do these things—to be at ease, actually to surrender, to take our time, to intend paradoxically by not intending. Yet this must be something radically more than an intellectual affirmation of belief in the Third Person of the Trinity in order to be an intellectually honest minister or professor. One must have a need that is uniquely his—the need for an Enabler and a capacity to *receive* help.

The Holy Spirit and Man's Capacity to Receive Gifts

The need to be self-sufficient underlies much of the anxiety which makes us inarticulate. The very use of words that have meaning implies the sharing of one's self with others and the confession of the need for others. The communication of love between husband and wife abounds in examples of this. The husband often feels that he has "said his say" when he has provided the material goods and opportunities his family needs. Yet they, and especially his wife, want him to "open up" and "say in words" how he feels about them. Conversely, the wife and mother may not sense her husband's and children's needs for *verbal* expression of her love in the form of appreciation, encouragement, and reflective interpretations of her and their relationships. Yet when these things are said, someone is prone to "change the subject quickly"! The capacity to receive the affection of others is itself a gift of the Holy Spirit. Crucial to our courage in the times of testing is the capacity not only to give but also to receive.

The capacity to receive the gift of the Spirit is never so great as when all other powers of life are depleted. H. Wheeler Robinson tells at the beginning of his book *The Christian Experience of the Holy Spirit* of a serious illness in which all his resources failed him. The gospel to him was all demand "for an active effort for which physical energy was lacking."[6] He was given the power and the words to produce his book. Through his own personal discovery of the ministry of the Holy Spirit, the book came into being. The adult's—not the child's—experience of helplessness is the precondition of the kind of openness, courage, and the generation of hope that comes through the Holy Spirit.

The Apostle Paul refined our whole conception of the ministry of articulation when he said:

. . . we rejoice in our sufferings, knowing that suffering produces endurance, and endurance produces character, and character produces hope, and hope does not disappoint us, because God's love has been poured into our hearts through the Holy Spirit which has been given to us (Romans 5:3–5).

But how can these things be if we cannot receive the given gift of the Holy Spirit? A story from Budapest, reported in 1961, speaks volumes as to all that has been said here:

"Internal emigration" is very much alive and active today in Budapest. There are many—the number is impossible to determine—who chose to "emigrate spiritually" from communism and remain physically at home after the 1956 revolt. People interested in intellectual and cultural affairs, and there are many in Budapest, seem to be aware of the comings and goings, the trials and tribulations, the triumphs and defeats of this group.

With the exception of Warsaw, there is no capital in Eastern Europe where writers, musicians and actors occupy so prominent a place in the public mind.

Nor do the intellectuals of the "internal emigration" miss an opportunity to let the Communist regime know where they stand. It is sometimes the aged and most honored who set an example of almost inviting the official world to do its worst.

A dramatic incident involving Zoltan Kodaly, Hungary's greatest living composer, epitomizes the attitude of the artists.

Mr. Kodaly was recently invited by the Communist officialdom to address an assembly of factory workers. The spare, 79-year old composer accepted the invitation. He arrived at the factory carrying a battered briefcase. Officials asked Mr. Kodaly what he was going to tell the workers. He replied curtly that this concerned only himself.

The composer mounted the rostrum, opened his briefcase and withdrew an old book. It was the Bible. His opening remarks were to the effect that he was not much of a hand at writing speeches and that he proposed to read what someone else had written. Mr. Kodaly then proceeded to read from the New Testament about brotherly love.[7]

(4)

The New Morality: A Psychological and Theological Critique

The contemporary psychologist of religion stands in a boundary situation as he considers the so-called "new" morality. His clinical approach binds him to real people caught in ambiguous choices between the lesser of two evils. On the one hand, he represents the ideals of the religious communities, and, on the other hand, he is called on to maintain a faithful relationship to other people and to himself, none of whom have achieved but all of whom have violated these ideals of the faith community.

Briefly defined, the "new" morality emphasizes the proximate as opposed to the ultimate nature of any moral code or principle. It accentuates the relativity of moral decisions to the exigencies of the situation in which these decisions are made. It suspends final judgments of right and wrong as it awaits fresh data which may confirm, invalidate, or modify a moral decision. The "new" morality relies heavily on rational deduction in decision-making and omits reference to the guidance of the Holy Spirit.

When this omission is not made, the work of the Holy Spirit is de-emphasized, to say the least.

In the hyphenations of the semanticists, the "new" morality is a "wait-and-see," "but-what-if," and "let's-get-down-to-cases" kind of morality.

The real misunderstanding of this "new" morality lies in the word *new* itself. This kind of morality is no ethical Melchizedek, without forebears or causes. The assumption of "newness" has led to a superficial "craze" in theological circles which, one fears, will be followed with exaggerated zeal for a short time. Then some other "new thing" will take its place with little regard for the dire consequences of the fad for that generation which took the "new" morality seriously.

One way of correcting this exaggerated zeal is to explore the background assumptions out of which the "new" morality and/or "situation ethics" have emerged. They did not spring "full-blown from the head of Zeus." They came from somewhere. A "situation" produced them. They in turn create a situation of their own which should be submitted to careful scrutiny.

Contemporary psychology can both correct and clarify the "new" morality by exploring its older assumptions and illuminating its serious history. Excessive zeal is often attributed to those who take the Holy Spirit seriously at the conscious level. Often this is true. However, another way to correct the exaggerated enthusiasm about the "new" morality is to pose and seek to answer the theological question as to the participation of the Holy Spirit in ethical decisions. Reference to the Holy Spirit may be viewed by the situation ethicist as an intuitional retreat from rationality in moral decision-making. However, a psychological and theological critique of the "new" morality will tend to take both the rational and the inspirational work of the Holy Spirit seriously. The critical and constructive reappraisal of the "new" morality from the point of view of the psychology of a "situation" and a theological relevance of the Holy Spirit to the situations, therefore, is the concern of this chapter.

The Holy Spirit and the Development of a Loving Conscience

The exponent of the "new" morality is Joseph A. Fletcher, in his book, *Situation Ethics: The New Morality*.[1] In his approaches to decision-making, Fletcher rejects the idolatry of codes by the legalist and the hedonism and self-seeking of the antinomian; and he espouses the situation ethic.

The situationist enters every decision-making situation fully armed with the ethical maxims of his community and its heritage, and he treats them with respect as illuminators of his problems. Just the same he is prepared in any situation to compromise them or set them aside *in the situation* if love seems better served by doing so.[2]

The decision to compromise or set aside a given ethical norm is made "by accepting reason as the instrument of moral judgment," and "by accepting revelation as the source of the norms while rejecting all 'revealed' norms or laws but one command—to love God in the neighbor."[3]

The major assumptions of reason and the love of God in ethical decisions, then, must be examined. These assumptions themselves rest on hidden presuppositions which Fletcher seems to ignore in a debonair naïveté. The first hidden assumption is *the use of the case history method.* He assumes the kind of disciplined person who knows how to use the case history method in making an ethical appraisal of a given situation. A "situation" is far more than a chance set of circumstances which can be analyzed quickly on the basis of rational guesswork by just any casual participant. The appraisal of a situation requires intensive discipline in the use of the case history method. The factual data of the long-term, contributing, and precipitating factors in a moral crisis was necessary for a full-orbed and reflective moral judgment. The "norms" themselves, as stated in biblical, legal, and folk-culture codes, are accumulated, case history upon case history. The "preparation" of the situation ethicist to compromise or set aside a given ethical norm requires that he be prepared in the use of the case history of a given situation as well as the larger history of the community of concern in which the events of a personal history take place. Fletcher does not give guidance in the art and science of this kind of clinical approach to decision-making. At the same time, he seems to assume that every "man in the street" has this kind of preparation in the use of the case history method. Likewise, Fletcher does not seem to be aware of the ways in which "situational" ethical decisions of yesterday themselves become the norms for ethical behavior today. One generation profits —or chooses not to profit—from the experience of previous generations. One must not only be "fully armed with the ethical maxims of his community and its heritage" as he makes ethical decision. He must also be thoroughly disciplined in how this "equipment" for the moral battle came into being, was put together, can be disassembled and reassembled, and kept clean for use.

A second hidden and unexamined assumption in the

"new" morality is the ethical dimensions of the principle of the development of personality. The case history method assumes the developmental process in human life. Ethical maturity is the forward intention of personality development. The use of reason, for example, in assessing a given ethical situation implies the use of intelligence. Intelligence itself is conditioned by the age factor. The age factor symbolizes growth and development. The degree of intelligence of a person, through innate endowment and cultural enrichment, conditions the kinds of compromises of ethical norms a person can make. The value system by which one is able to express his love for God in his neighbor takes the skillful tailoring of disciplined intelligence. The developmental process itself depends upon the person's *capacity* to grow and the degree of moral responsibility he is capable of accepting.

For example, legal jurisprudence and prudential ethics distinguish moral responsibility on an age factor basis. Some offenders are called juvenile delinquents and others adult offenders. Even within the church and in theology the nature of sin is assessed in terms of "the age of accountability."

An act of a five-year-old child, for example, is ethically different when it is performed by a fifteen-year-old adolescent. In turn, the fifteen-year-old's behavior is ethically different from the same act performed by a thirty-five-year-old adult. If the same behavior persists as a habit without change in a person over a period of forty years from the time he or she is four or five, this is ethically different from the same act being performed only three times— once at five, once at fifteen, and once at thirty-five—without continual repetition in between. An example is the homosexual act. Even the habitual act of a person is different if performed in privacy and fantasy as over against being taught to others. Such ethical distinctions as these are based upon the assumption of the cumulative record of a life story. The situational ethics of Fletcher assume such developmental concepts but do not specify them.

When one turns to the Scripture, he reads the gospel speaking of love as being strong meat for the mature and the law as "the milk" of the word for the immature. The gospel is thought of as the advanced, adult expression of the intention of God in Christ. The law is spoken of as the "tutor" that prepares the person for the gospel. The "new" morality, it seems to me, "edits out" these presuppositions of the levels of maturity in the deciding person. The situation ethicist seems to assume that "every man knows best for him." The end result is that each man is encouraged to do what is right in his own eyes, regardless of his particular level of intelligence, age, capacity of perception, and discipline in decision-making.

This leads to a third hidden assumption in the new morality—that the "love of God in the neighbor" is full-blown in its maturity in all persons. The Apostle Paul prayed for the Philippians that their love might increase "more and more, with knowledge and all discernment" (Philippians 1:9). The hymn to love in the thirteenth chapter of First Corinthians speaks of love as an adult way of thinking, speaking, and acting. It requires that men put away childish things. In Ephesians "speaking the truth in love" is associated with "growing up" in Christ. Love is not anywhere assumed in the New Testament to be a "logically given," either in creation or in redemption, whereby the rational capacity of man inevitably works properly in decision-making.

Rather, love is biblically expressed as a gift-in-embryo of the Holy Spirit. Through the exercise of the gifts of apostleship, evangelism, shepherding, and teaching, the saints are equipped for the work of ministry. They all attain unto mature manhood by speaking the truth in love. Thus they grow up into the headship of Christ. Christian love is not only the gift-in-embryo of the Holy Spirit; love is also the first fruit of maturity of the Holy Spirit. The fruits of the Spirit are ethical fruits—"love, joy, peace, patience, kindness . . . gentleness, self-control; against such there is no law" (Galatians 5:22–23). If one is led by the Spirit he is not under the law. The criterion of such leadership is not some ecstatic inspirationalism. It is participation in the crucifixion of Jesus Christ (Galatians 5:18, 24). Renewal of the moral life takes place through the acceptance of the discipline of the Cross of Jesus Christ. The "pouring" of God's love into our hearts through the Holy Spirit produces a hope that does not disappoint us (Romans 15:13). This focuses the ethical process of development of personality in the indwelling work of the Holy Spirit. William Temple summarized it well:

The greatest of all the opportunities there is, or ever can be, in the world is to know the character of God . . . and so to know it that our hearts are called out in sympathy so that we not only do His Will thinking it must be sensible to do what He wants, but that we want to do it. That will to do it, in the heart of man, that is the Holy Spirit.[4]

I asked Joseph Fletcher what role he felt the Holy Spirit performs in the ethical assessment of a given situation. He said:

This is an important issue posed by situational theory to theological ethics. There are four approaches to understanding the process of moral choice: (1) the intuitional approach of Rudolf Otto which assumes a built-in radar or "faculty" of moral choice; (2) the inspirational approach which assumes that the Holy Spirit comes from the outside of man and guides him; (3) the rationalist approach of the Thomist which assumes that conscience is reason at work making moral judgments; (4) the introjectionist approach which assumes that moral choices are made by the introjected commands of past moral supervisors such as parents and teachers.

Fletcher took his stand with the rationalists and rejected the other three. With reference to the Holy Spirit, he said: "I really do not think you have said anything when you say that the Holy Spirit is at work in human decision. On this I am an agnostic." This is a strange contradiction of his written remark when he says that the *agape* kind of love of which he speaks is the Holy Spirit.[5] Here he almost directly quotes William Temple, who said:

All the great theologians have always said that the love wherewith a man loves God or his neighbor is the Holy Ghost. It is not the *work* of the Holy Ghost only, it *is* the Holy Ghost. It is God, the supreme, eternal, universal spirit at work in the hearts of His creature.[6]

Neither in his book nor under the pressure of questioning is Fletcher this clear. He says he is agnostic as to the Holy Spirit. He says that love *is* the Holy Spirit. In fact, one wonders if his doctrine of God is either unitarian or binitarian, but has no way of telling which he believes. One could as easily say that God is love. Therefore, he could dispense with either the Second or the Third Person of the Trinity. The core criticism of Fletcher, then, is basically a christological one. I grant that a twentieth-century perception of the Trinity that is communicable and clear is needed. But one asks whether Fletcher is not rejecting the superstitious images awakened in him by the mention of the Holy Spirit. One asks with Paul Tillich concerning the ethicists of our day:

Will it ever again be possible to say without theological embarrassment or mere conformity to tradition the great words, "In the name of the Father, the Son, and the Holy Spirit"? Or will it be possible again to pray for blessings through "the love of God, the Father, and the grace of Jesus Christ and the fellowship of the Holy Spirit" without awakening superstitious images in those who hear the prayer? I believe it is possible. . . .[7]

When Fletcher says that the love of God in the neighbor is the criterion of rational judgments of ethical situations, he implicitly excludes the Holy Spirit from access to man's reasonable judgments. This cuts the theological rootage of his ethical theory by excluding the nonrational portions of man's being. Thus consciousness is narrowed. Inevitably the fruits of such an anthropology will shrivel. The situation ethics Fletcher espouses is a theological "cut flower" —beautiful for the moment but destined to shrivel. From a psychological perspective, Fletcher's rationalism ignores the developmental process of ethical maturity. At the same time he assumes the use of the case history method. From an historical point of view, he assumes Thomas Aquinas's conclusions of rationalism without attention to the Thomistic presuppositions of authority. Thomas Aquinas himself said that the law is "an ordination of reason promulgated for the common good by him who has the care of the community."[8] This trivializes the relationship between the immanent indwelling of God in the Holy Spirit. The Holy Spirit is not some sort of *external* control. The very process of development itself is the power and direction of the Holy Spirit. Love is both the gift-in-embryo and the first fruit of the Holy Spirit. Ignoring both the developmental process and the reality of the Holy Spirit seem to be related to each other as cause and effect. The mature ethical decisions of a Christian in any situation are the developed results of the Holy Spirit. As Eric Rust has aptly said:

. . . the Holy Spirit represents the immanence of God in his universe. The Father is God as the ground of creative and redemptive power, the Son or Word is the personal activity of God coming forth in creative and redemptive love, and the Holy Spirit is the immanent aspect of the love effecting the divine purpose in nature and history, and especially in the life of the redeemed man.[9]

The Psychological Background of Situationism in Morality

Psychologists of personality for the past thirty years have been devising theoretical models of human persons in relation to each other. These models reflect the complex nature of a "situation." Older theorists of personality took the clues of developmentalism and the cumulative case history from Darwinian evolution and Freudian geneticism. Biology was the parent science of these nineteenth-century scientists of culture and personality. Physics and nuclear theory provide the parent science of the more recent models of personality.

A Situation as "Life Space": Kurt Lewin

In 1936 Kurt Lewin said: "One can hope to understand the forces that govern behavior only if one includes in the

representation the whole psychological situation." He said
that Dostoievsky gave us "the most complete and concrete
descriptions of situations." Dostoievsky showed us "in a
definite way how the different facts in an individual's
environment are related to each other and to the individual himself." Lewin spoke of inventories and systems
of behavior within a situation which he named the "life
space" of a person. By this he meant the "totality of
possible events" in a person's life. Instead of classifying
kinds of behavior as "possible" or "not possible," one
must derive his judgment of a given kind of action from
the *totality* of "possibles." This derivation cannot be
determined externally or partially; it must be derived from
within the life space of an individual and from the life
space "as a whole." This shifts the stress in evaluating
behavior from objects to processes, from states of being to
changes of states of being. Lewin summarized:

> If the life space is a totality of possible events, then "things"
> that enter the situation, especially the person himself and
> psychological "objects," have to be characterized by their re-
> lationship to possible events.[10]

Lewin shifted from the Aristotelian mode of rationalism
and classification of behavior to a Heraclitean appreciation of process and a Galileo-like grasp of the totality of
life as being more than a collection of unrelated events. In
this view, "situation" was defined as the powerful inter-
play of an action and "reaction," as a complex field of
reciprocal relations within and between persons. The
momentary situation and life situation were distinguished
from, but inseparably related to, each other as event and
history. A purely rational classification of behavior as
isolated act apart from the total life space or situation was

thus consigned to pre-nineteenth-century conceptions of science. The relativity of the galaxies of the starry heavens above to each other now became the relativity of the moral laws within, to paraphrase Immanuel Kant. The "situation" of human behavior, to be perceived at all, had to be perceived in its totality. Lewin used this concept to devise ways of "resolving social conflicts" and operational approaches to group life. The rich inner diversity of Lewin's conception of the "situation" stands in contrast to the "situation" of which Fletcher speaks. Fletcher excludes portions of man's being from the assessment of a moral situation—he writes off intuition and the influences that "come from the outside" of a person. He falls into the trap of a "faculty psychology" in which "reason" is supreme at the same time he rejects Otto as an intuitionalist. The Lewinian grasp after the totality of the life space of a person is a far more adequate and contemporary understanding of what a "situation" is in the first place.

Situationism and Field Theory: Gardner Murphy

A second formulation of situationism in morality is found in the first edition of Gardner Murphy's book *Personality: A Biosocial Approach to Origins and Structure,* published in 1947. Murphy entitles one of his chapters "Situationism." Situationism means that "human beings respond as situations require them to respond; and that whatever their biological diversities, they will, if capable of learning, take on the attributes which the situations call for."[11] Some such adaptations to situations are instantaneous; others take time for learning. Murphy uses the situation of one's roles in life and the reciprocal effect that role change has on personality and vice versa, particularly upon one's value structure and ethical decisions. For example, a certain minister in a conventional church situation *as minister*, when asked whether a divorced person should remarry, will tend to respond unequivocally with a No. The same minister, asked to remarry his divorced mother or sister when he is visiting at home during the summer vacation, is likely to equivocate. He does so for more reasons than one: (1) he is in the role of a son or brother and not just that of a minister; (2) he is in a different field of relationships with different commitments; (3) he responds more existentially and less in terms of a stereotyped set of expectations. A moral imperative for ministers in their accustomed roles can be derived from this that will tend to transcend situations: When a minister gives guidance to a person on ethical matters, would he be willing to give the same guidance to his nearest of kin? This catches personality at its heart, and ethical decisions thus made tend to be more authentic because they express the totality of the life space of the minister. He is not just playing *a* role. He is expressing his whole being in a demanding situation. Murphy, therefore, defines personality "as the locus of intersection of *all* the roles he [the individual] enacts"; the age roles, sex roles, occupational roles, marital roles, parental roles, and the national and religious roles are confronted at the point of their consistency with each other.

Murphy's perspective clarifies many of Joseph Fletcher's dilemma situations, such as that of the beautiful girl on the plane who has been asked to use her sexual charms to elicit security information for her government. She raises the question in terms of her national role—as an American citizen—and her family role—as one whose brother is in the military risking his life. Why could

Fletcher not have answered her in terms of demands *other* than that of her government—such as the wishes of her brother, her expectations of marriage in the future, and her relationship to Fletcher as a minister? Instead he answers her by disavowing his knownness to her as a minister-confessor and condemns her for trusting him as a stranger! He says: "I do not think you should take the espionage assignment because you have trusted me, a total stranger, with your dilemma and I do not think a person who trusts strangers should be entrusted with our national security!" This is a clever, "perfect-squelch" answer, but it represents a superficial and partial evaluation of the demands of the girl's life situation and her conflicting roles. Where is the point of convergence of all her roles? Where is the point of convergence of all Fletcher's roles? For example, would he want an older Episcopal clergyman in whom a member of his family confides to answer her this way in her time of ethical dilemma? In this instance we may have met Fletcher as a professor answering a question in a classroom jousting match. We have not met the complete Fletcher responding totally to the demands of a crucial life situation.

Murphy, furthermore, gives even more specific guidance on situationism in ethics in his discussion of field theory. Physicists found very early that they could "no longer explain events by referring to the interaction of parts that push and pull; each event came to be conceived as an aspect of a field of events."[12] In the face of field theory, along with the leadership of Lewin, Sullivan, Angyal, and others, Murphy says that "the situationist has become a field theorist, and field theory is a point of view which has just [in 1947] been developed."[13] Field theory pointed at that time to the developed inner organization of personality which, in addition to responding to a situation, was capable of resisting the demands of a given situation. Not only does a person resist the demands of the situation, but the intrusion of a given personality into a situation makes him what Sullivan called in the 1950's "a participant observer," one who both is changed by the situation and changes it by his very presence in it. The reciprocity between the self and its phenomenal field is a continuum and not a sharp demarcation of individual and environment. Neither polarity of the field can be taken for granted, the situation itself nor the inner resistance to the situation. Both must be carefully studied as to their strengths "as an expression of all the forces in the field."[14]

In the particular individual personality, Murphy contended, "life depends, to a large degree, on relatively irreversible *commitments,* and each commitment constitutes a field. . . . field determination goes deep; and when once a commitment has been made, there is usually no possibility of going back to the unformed stage."[15] Although internal consistency and irreversibility may be a reality, facades of "private" and "public" attitudes may be maintained. Even so, however, the underlying commitment remains. A person, "after functioning in a field may not escape it and go back, scot-free, to an earlier undifferentiated outlook." Thus a new element is introduced by field theory into the matter of ethical decision: *commitments.*

Commitment and the Transcendence of Situations

Any assessment of the new morality and the norms which would illuminate the decision-making processes in concrete situations must add to its data the kinds of prior commitments which a person brings to the decision. The power of previous covenants will tend to determine behavior even when the conscious decision is to the contrary. The most common example of this is the way in which ingrained instructions of the Roman Catholic Church for generations concerning birth control will tend to determine the sexual behavior of a couple after marriage, regardless of their so-called rational, enlightened compromise or setting aside of the church rulings about contraception.

The codes and norms of the Old and New Testaments are set within a larger framework of covenants or commitments. The observance of codes and norms may be irrational, even ridiculous to the communicant, but the commitments and covenants that their observance symbolizes may be extremely serious and provide the code with its power. Not all law is dead. A given legal expectation of a person may be enlivened by the kinds of commitments he has made and which the law symbolizes. For example, the *reasons* for keeping the Sabbath tend to shift in the different codes and historical situations of the Old Testament. Exodus 20:8–11 cites the reason as the resting of the Lord after the Creation, but Deuteronomy 6:12–15 cites the same reason and adds a new one—the rescue of the Israelites from the slave labor camps of Egypt. The Christian observance of the Lord's Day builds upon sabbatarian practice but shifts the nature of the commitment to the celebration of the Resurrection of the Christ. The element of commitment and covenant is a situation-transcending basis for ethical decision. These commitments give ethical decision an "independence" of situation, even though the independence and defiance of a situation by an individual would have little meaning apart from the situation against which he protests. Therefore, Murphy says that field theory moves on a continuum and not a cleft "either-or-ishness" between ethical rigidity and compliance in a given situation. Even so,

> It is important to recognize the personality which can shut off much of the outer world, can overpower others, or can make real to itself aspects of the field that mean little to others. We may call it the "gyroscopic" personality, for it goes on spinning in its own way in spite of the pitching and rolling of the deck on which it stands.[16]

It seems ironic that the flashing paperback of today is entitled *Situation Ethics: The New Morality.* Not long ago the "in" book was David Riesman's *Lonely Crowd.* The appeal then was for the "inner-directed" rather than the "other-directed" man. The field theorist would emphasize the importance of both the situation of the committed person and his capacity to be an "inner-directed" man and to resist and change a situation. Without this, the popular paperback of tomorrow will be entitled *The Uncommitted Man.*

Andras Angyal, a research psychiatrist, took the field theory of Lewin, Sullivan, and Murphy seriously in a book published in 1965. He said life's commitments take place within the *biosphere* of life. By this he meant the total sphere of life with its autonomous and homonomous trends, i.e., its self-directed and other-directed trends, which are inseparable from each other. He said that the commitment of a person may take a heavily autonomous trend with a set of fixed, safe *rules to live by.* Another protective device is to make "sharp arbitrary divisions . . . combined with a species of desperate dogmatism which arbitrarily *overshouts doubt.*" On another pattern of defense against wholeheartedness by "a life style of *uncommitment*," Angyal wrote:

He refuses to take responsibility in the sense of identifying himself with his actions and saying unequivocally, "Here I stand." The person is always eyeing two possibilities, choosing a little of both, but neither completely. In this way he turns his life into a farce and deprives himself of real fulfillment. He usually feels that in avoiding commitments he leads a brave fight for personal freedom, but since he does not use it when he has it the fight turns out to be a fight for the freedom to sit on the fence.[17]

The new morality hastens to extol the ethical chameleon, who adapts to any situation. Yet there is need for some rather stubborn beavers who will chew into their wooded situation rather than blend with it. But, as Murphy says:

Never does the purest beaver become self-contained, ignoring the difference between trees; never does the most volatile chameleon lose the inner individuality which distinguishes him from other chameleons.[18]

In both instances, the prior commitments make the difference in ethical choice, for

It is the promises we make that keep us awake,
It is the promises we keep that help us sleep.

Fletcher speaks of compromise of norms in order that the love of God in neighbor may be effected in a given decision. The very word *compromise* itself has become a dirty word in our language. But its etymology points to a defective superficiality in situational ethics and the new morality. *Compromise* literally means to do something "with a promise." Ethical decisions are made in terms of the promises one has already made. An ethical decision *is* a new promise that constitutes a new field in one's ongoing life purpose. An ethical decision has as its hormic, or purposive, goal the creation of new hope or promise for living the future. Life, after a good decision, looks promising. The giving of commandment *with promise,* such as honoring one's father and mother, brings with it the hope that one's own days may be long in the land the Lord his God has given him. This element of promise and commitment, hope and freedom from despair, is the "gyroscopic" element in ethical decisions which transcends situations. This element seems to be missing in the "new" morality. If it is not missing, it remains hidden as an assumption.

Covenant Ethics Versus Situational Ethics

The kind of covenant or promise which provides both balance and direction for Christian ethics and pastoral leadership needs identification, dramatization, and celebration. This covenant was established in the redemptive act of Jesus Christ. Christ set us free for freedom from the law. But in doing so, he bound us with the bonds of a commitment, not to a dead law, but to a Living Redeemer. Yet even the teachings of Jesus himself can be taken as laws apart from the redemption and forgiveness provided in the new testament of his sacrificial death. Both early and late accounts of his departure from his disciples record the kinds of promises he made to them and the kinds of commitments he expected from them as the bases of their later actions. These promises and commitments given and taken became the dynamic field of relationship which we know as the church, the living Body of Christ. The guideline for ethical action was to love one another as he has loved us. This was the "new" commandment.

The prophets and the law hung on the commandment to love God and one's neighbor. There was nothing new in this. The new element in Christian ethics was that right action springs from the specific covenant of loving one another as Christ loved the church and gave himself up for it. Lest this itself become a dead law, Christ *promised* his disciples the gift of the Holy Spirit. His promise was fulfilled. He created a new field of powerful interaction known as the church. The pouring out of the Holy Spirit brought into vital being the reality of the church of the believers in the resurrected Christ. The gift of the Holy Spirit established this covenanted community. This is the situation of the Christian as he makes moral decision. As T. S. Eliot said, even the anchorite in the desert prays in terms of this community.

Such decisions do not allow men the luxury of the freedom to sit on the fence, as Angyal says. Nor do they permit the aesthetic contemplation of omnipotence as if we were Olympian gods with *all* alternatives at our total disposal. Telford Taylor describes the situation precisely when he speaks of the German Army in the first months of World War II:

The conquests of the Wehrmacht were awesome, but the combination of decisions that led to them were military madness. He who cannot reject cannot select, and the downfall of the Third Reich was due, in no small measure, to Adolf Hitler's inability to realize that, in strategic terms, the road to everywhere is the road to nowhere.[19]

For a fellowship to become genuine and effective, decision must be made. The effort at inclusion, which is such a wholesome corrective of the exclusiveness of Christian groups, cannot establish the integrity without some clear-cut rejection of the schematizations of the world disorder around it. The gathered fellowship of believers then becomes a field of both resistance to and accommodation with the world of which it has always been a part. The "company of the committed" has been debtor to both the chameleons and the beavers of whom Murphy spoke. Yet the persistent corrective of legalism has been the renewal of the church through the gift of the Holy Spirit. The reality of the Holy Spirit cannot be restricted to the "outside" or the "inside" of men's ethical processes.

The power of the promise of the Holy Spirit commands a response—an ethical response. As such we are enabled to become a self that transcends the situation. This happened, happens, and will continue to happen. A self transcends a situation. In Robert Bolt's *A Man For All Seasons* Sir Thomas More, facing death for resisting the "situation" of Henry VIII, when "administrative convenience" would have required only that he "look the other way," nevertheless says to his daughter:

When a man takes an oath, Meg, he's holding his own self in his own hands. Like water. And if he opens his fingers *then*—he needn't hope to find himself again. Some men aren't capable of this, but I'd be loathe to think your father one of them.[20]

The Holy Spirit in an
Age of Administration

Administration is a taboo word among theologians, pastors, and an increasing number of lay churchmen. The word has many negative connotations. Its signal reaction value among such persons is hardly surpassed by any other word. One begins to suspect that a word like this could not arouse such emotion unless considerable repression and lack of personal insight were not in progress. For example, one finds theological students rejecting the role of pastor and taking positions in such government projects as the antipoverty program. They seem to feel that in doing so they are getting away from the large amount of "administration" a pastor has to do. One finds ministers wanting to enter the institutional or military chaplaincy in order "to work with people" and not have so much administration to do. Yet if we look at such moves with hard-nosed realism we see that they are like the man who "fled from a lion, and a bear met him; or went into the house and leaned with his hand against the wall, and a serpent bit him" (Amos 5:19).

This is an age of administration. We have shifted from the era of the "great man theory" of leadership to that of the "organization man" theory of leadership. My premise is this: The Holy Spirit as the entempled activity of God among men can and does transform an organization that would otherwise be felt as a machine into an organism that contributes to and sustains the personal growth of the men and women in it. As William H. Whyte says, "To say that we must recognize the dilemmas of organization society is not to be inconsistent with the hopeful premise that organization society can be as compatible for the individual as any previous society."[1] Avoiding administration is impossible; investing administration with a distinctly religious meaning and purpose is a pressing "preface to sustained individuality in an age of administration." The purpose of this chapter is to explore the distinctly religious dimensions of administration. The Holy Spirit in relation to the "gift of administration" is the way to insight into the religious identity of the administrator. Hence, I have chosen to approach this subject from the point of view of the Holy Spirit in an age of administration.

Three New Testament concepts provide a profile for a religious meaning of administration. This meaning in turn provides a frame of reference for the work of the administrator as an agent of the Holy Spirit in the leadership of the flock of God.

The first concept of administration in the New Testament is that of *ministering*. The Greek word for this is *diakoneo;* the literal meaning is to "wait upon others," as in waiting upon tables. More metaphorically, this points to the "patience motive" as well as the "service motive" in administration. The power to serve patiently is coupled with the power to "wait" upon others with one's own goals "bracketed in" until their's have been expressed.

The second New Testament concept of administration is that of *sharing in the corporate life*. The Greek word for it is *koinoneo;* literally this means "distributing" charitably of one's goods, but more metaphorically it means communicating with others and forming a community of shared responsibility of its members for and with each other. It involves intimacy. In some of its connotations the word is used to refer to the most intimate of human encounters in sexual response.

A third concept for administration in the New Testament is that of *reflective observation and sustained attention to the total life of a people together*. The Greek word for this is *episkopeo;* its literal meaning is "hitting the mark" or "having good aim," as in marksmanship. Its more metaphorical meaning is having good judgment, wide perspective, and the capacity to inspect, analyze, decide, and oversee to completion a given set of relationships. The vertical dimension of this metaphor is that of "watching over the visitation of God to his people."

These three concepts can be summarized: The administrator is an *initiator* who creates new possibilities in old forms. He is a *perpetuator* who sees to it that these are carried through to completion. He is a *distributor* who makes sure that both power and responsibility are shared by those who are subject to the decisions being effected. He is the one who keeps his aim when others lose theirs. He maintains perspective of the totality of corporate relationships when other persons' perspective becomes partial and segmented. He is a *disciplinarian* who calls the hand of other men's measliness in behalf of the common good. As such, he is, in summary, the *overseer* of the flock of God. What then is the relationship of the Holy Spirit to the overseer, or administrator, of the flock of God?

The Holy Spirit is the counselor, the director, and the

energizer of the administrator as an overseer of the flock of God. Psychology and psychotherapy can inform the administrator's understanding of the work of the Holy Spirit amid his own function as an overseer of the flock of God. In this chapter the biblical understanding of the work of the Holy Spirit and the task of the overseer of the flock of God will be brought into polar relationship with some of the best that psychological understandings of man have to offer to us today. By analogy, the power of the Holy Spirit is transformed into light for the living of these days through both the *psyche* of man and the imperishable work of God in Jesus Christ, recorded through the Holy Writ. As two carbon bars, electrified by thrusts of current, brought into right relation to each other produce light, even so light breaks forth when we bring biblical knowledge into dialogue with psychological knowledge at the point of the administrator's function as an overseer of the flock of God.

The Holy Spirit and the Function of Administration

John D. Maguire says that Jesus "has a preoccupation with verbs: come, follow, taste, see, love, suffer, become. He appears unconcerned with definitions."[2] The concern of this chapter is in that tradition, i.e., with the verb, the act, the function of overseeing. This is not to ignore the importance of the *office* or *status* of the overseer in the New Testament even. Rather, it is to deal with the functional dimensions of overseeing rather than the ecclesiological. This is based upon the hypothesis of structural offices, i.e., that their validity lies in their exercise and not their occupation as offices.

When we take this approach to overseeing, we see that

the biblical verb means "to look at, take care, and to see to a matter," as in Hebrews 12:15–16. The overseer is to "see to it that no one fail to obtain the grace of God; that no 'root of bitterness' spring up and cause trouble, and by it many become defiled; that no one be immoral or irreligious like Esau, who sold his birthright for a single meal." Overseeing, then, means caring for the individuals who stand in need of the grace of God, guarding the fellowship of Christians, in which bitterness may become a defilement of the whole flock of God, and shortsighted reaches for immediate security may plunge an individual or group into immorality.

Paul, in speaking to the elders at Ephesus, linked this function of overseeing with the work of the Holy Spirit. He said in Acts 20:28: "Take heed to yourselves and to all the flock, in which the Holy Spirit has made you guardians [*episkopous*], to feed the church of the Lord which he obtained with his own blood." *To feed* here accents the shepherding of the flock, and translates the same word from which we get our word *pastor*. Administration, then, involves the "shared appraisal" of the flock of God and the shepherd of the flock in determining together who are the men "from among their own selves who speak perverse things and draw away the disciples after them." No artificial distinction is drawn here between the sustaining and disciplinary tasks of the administrator. They are held in a unified function—one as a shepherding perspective and the other as an organizational perspective, to rely upon Seward Hiltner's concepts.[3] The work of the Holy Spirit accounts for the unity of both the overseeing function and the fellowship of the church of the Lord which Christ obtained with his own blood.

The real question, then, is this: "In what ways does the

Holy Spirit bring unity, clarity, and effectiveness to the administrator of the flock of God?"

Developing Spiritual Resonance

The coming of the Holy Spirit at Pentecost caused each man to hear the Apostles in his own language. Within the delicate mystery of the people's capacities to grasp the totality of what was happening, a miracle occurred. Each was able to capture the meaning of the other. There was a subsoil of devoutness in the audience. The text says that those who were present were "devout men from every nation under heaven." Earl Loomis, a New York psychoanalyst, has called the process of nonverbal, subverbal, and superverbal understanding *resonance*. Of course, its opposite is *dissonance*. One can by analogy see this in the reaction of music instruments to each other. For example, two tuning forks of the same kind will both vibrate when one is struck. Among human beings the *consciousness of kind*, or the feeling of kinship, produces a sympathetic vibration between people. The gift of the Holy Spirit energizes this kind of understanding between people who are in deep fellowship with each other. This understanding is highly idiosyncratic—each understands in his own way. It is highly communal—those who understand each other eat together in gladness and singleness of heart. This understanding is reciprocal—no one person is left to do all the understanding in one-way communication. Reuel Howe calls this reciprocity "dialogue."

Dialogue . . . is more than communication. It is communion in which we have been mutually informed, purified, illumined, and reunited to ourselves, to one another, and God. A spirit pervades and directs the "conversation," and from this spirit, which Christians believe was fully incarnate in Christ, comes the fruits of the Spirit. Dialogue is a condition and relationship for the appearance and work of his Spirit, which calls men to, and enables them for, dialogue out of which comes the fruits of dialogue of the Spirit.[4]

The administrator of the flock of God has primary responsibility to be a *resonator* of the Holy Spirit. By definition a resonator receives with true fidelity the impulses of the original tone and intensifies it that all may hear. The administrator is, or should be, related in this way to the Holy Spirit on the one hand and to the flock of God on the other. In this function others may have a choice to be or not to be. The committed ones who have been charged to tend the flock of God have by personal choice decided to eliminate this option. As such, the administrator is the active instrumentality of the Holy Spirit. Gabriel Marcel states the hazards of this instrumentality well:

To be instrumental is, by definition, to be at the service of powers that are not themselves instrumental. . . . We are being the very nature of such powers when we seek to embody them for the purposes of imagination, for as soon as we do we reduce them to mere instruments.[5]

The administrator therefore looks first to himself as to whether he is using the Holy Spirit to produce a magic trick of his own or whether he has renounced the hidden things of ungodliness wherein he would seek to "use" the Holy Spirit. In this sense, the personal relationship of the administrator is more that of a wizard than that of a shepherd, more of an "operator" than a resonator of that Power not himself. As a resonator of the Holy Spirit, however, his task is to bring estranged portions of himself, persons within the fellowship, and persons outside the fellowship into resonant understanding and reciprocal conversation on a face-to-face basis.

The Assimilation of New and Strange Experience

The second function of the Holy Spirit in the life and work of the administrator is the creative assimilation of new and strange experiences on the part of individual Christians and the fellowship of believers as a total community of faith. Here the work of the administrator comprises both a personal counseling ministry and a ministry of reconciliation in the great dilemmas created by dynamic social change both within and without the church. Both the individual and the community are called upon to absorb, assimilate, and incorporate new ideas, experiences, and people which are alien to their selves as they know themselves.

Contemporary psychotherapists have not changed the character of human nature in its action and reaction in relation to the assimilation of the "new" and the "unheard-of" in life. They have, however, informed us with working hypotheses that illuminate our approach to such crises. Erik Erikson calls such incursions of new experience "crises in identity." The integrity of the individual and the community is at stake. The question is literally "Will I (or we) be held together or will I (we) be torn asunder?" Erikson says there are two dimensions to the crisis of identity: discontinuity and continuity. The person or community must make a break with old structures, mores, accepted patterns of thinking. This must be a clean break so that he and those around him will know that something new has happened. Yet, Erikson says, there must be continuity, in that the person stays in clear touch with his past and takes upon himself the responsibility of making it clear to his community what he has discovered and wants to become.[6] This could as well apply to the community of faith which develops a new sense of mission as a church and yet maintains with love its heritage. This has, since Marcion, been the decision of the people of the New Testament in relation to those of the Old Testament. Without *both* continuity and discontinuity, the individual and community are thrown into conflict which may be creative or destructive, benign or malignant.

The Gestalt psychologists have been helpful here, too. For example, Andras Angyal speaks of the tendency in individual and community toward complete realization of its own totality. The task of the administrator, from our perspective here, "is not to find direct relations between items but to find the superordinate system in which they are connected or to define their positional value within a system."[7] This is a reapplication of a concept of Angyal, who falls into the Gestalt patterning of life view. Within the total configuration of a personality or a community, Angyal says, changes do not occur from part to part of the total system but *"from a part to the whole or from the whole to a part."* He continues by suggesting ways in which the individual or the community becomes disturbed and sick. New experiences, unassimilated, can become "competitive systems, resulting in inevitable *mutual interference of systems."* In this instance, *pressure* is brought upon the leading system, acting-out behavior may *intrude* upon the leading system, or real pathology may take place in the mutual invasion or *intrusion* of one system upon another.

Angyal also says that new experiences and unassimilated concerns of the total system may be handled by *segregation of systems*. Here the difficulty is localized in such a way that the whole system is not threatened. To quote Angyal exactly: "We refer to this difference in daily life when we say that one person is doing something 'halfheartedly' and another is involved 'body and soul.' "[8]

Experiences and ideas may be so totally unacceptable that they remain unassimilated in any sense. Here the individual or the community as a whole becomes totally disturbed by the part. Angyal says that in an ideal individual or community, the "various part processes are integrated in such a way that they subserve and promote the total function or the organism." When a part rises up and rules the whole (to paraphrase Plato's definition of *sin*) this becomes what Angyal calls *bionegativity,* which he defines as *"a personality constellation in which one or more part processes disturb the total function of the organism."*[9]

The reader may wonder: "What has this to do with the Holy Spirit and the task of administration?" With imagination one can easily turn to the Damascus road experience of the Apostle Paul and see one that was so new to him that it blinded him. Ananias, who baptized him, must have done much to help him assimilate and comprehend what had happened to him. But the Jewish community back at Jerusalem could never absorb this man and his experience into a higher synthesis and totality. One has only to read Romans 9:1–5 to sense the grief Paul felt about being cut off from the Jews and his willingness to be cut off from Christ himself if they could be united in Christ. For the Christian community itself many years of patient testing of Paul and instruction by Barnabas were required before they could hear the Holy Spirit say to the church at Antioch, "Set apart for me Barnabas and Saul for the work to which I have called them" (Acts 13:2).

Then arose the great social dilemma of the relationship of the Jewish Christians to the Gentiles. They sat silently and listened to Paul and Barnabas concerning their work with the Gentiles. The community as a whole was coming to grips in the Jerusalem conference with assimilating the Gentiles with the Jews in the Christian faith. The conference itself decided not to trouble those of the Gentiles who turned to God. In doing so, Paul and Barnabas activated their task, not just as missionaries, but as ministers of reconciliation who served as administrators of the whole community. The words of the conference to the Gentiles were that they were to abstain from idols, from unchastity, and "from what is strangled and from blood." However, they did not become aware, it seems, that they themselves were a new and unassimilated experience within Judaism. They concluded their injunctions by saying: "For from early generations Moses has had in every city those who preach him, for he is read every sabbath in the synagogues" (Acts 15:21).

The contemporary pastor, or shepherdly administrator, deals with similar dilemmas. He is forced to come to terms with the earlier covenants that brought his church into being. At the same time, he seeks to develop the kinds of understanding that will keep new emphases within the church—such as racial integration—from being either rejected by the church or given full reign to bring division or destruction into the solidarity of the community of faith. This cannot be done by cleverness and manipulation, although this is not to say that human intelligence rightly committed is not acutely needed. The Holy Spirit "works things together" when the time is right, and the Holy Spirit requires of committed persons the wisdom to discern the emergence of new forms of life within the individual as well as in the church as a whole.

One useful analogy is that of growth in the body. If the normal process of assimilation and digestion goes on as it should, the body grows, not a part at a time, but totally. Growth in any part comes simultaneously with commensurate growth in every other part. If this is not true, then a neoplasm, or new organism, begins to grow parasitically on the rest of the body. This may be a benign growth or it may be malignant, but in either instance it is unassimilated.

If indeed the church is the Body of Christ, and we are members one of another, it seems accurate to apply the analogy to the church and its members. The Holy Spirit entemples himself within each of us. Our task is to be comprehensively related to the whole as being its members. The inspiration of the Holy Spirit is to edify, or build up, not to divide and set every man against his brother. The committed administrator prays for this. Yet he must take into consideration the new things that God yet has to reveal to us through the Holy Spirit after the manner of his revelation of himself in Jesus Christ. Therefore, the genuine administrator can be distinguished from the false prophet by his concern for the individual in relation to and not in isolation from the total Body of Christ. Attestations of leadership by the Holy Spirit which come to the working pastor can be tested by the willingness of the individual to have his "revelations" tested by time within a community in relation to the whole community. For example, churches are quick to ordain men to the ministry without such testing of time and durable relationship to the community of the believers. Conversely, the fellowship of the whole community must be extremely alert when a minority of even *one* person protests. Neither minority nor majority rule was the index of group action in the early church. Rather, the Scripture says that "they were all together in one place. . . . And they were all filled with the Holy Spirit and began to speak in other tongues, as the Spirit gave them utterance. . . . and they were bewildered, because each one heard them speaking in his own language" (Acts 2:1, 4, 6). The Holy Spirit brought them gladness and singleness of heart. They looked to the Holy Spirit for understanding and communion of spirit instead of to each other for a head count as to whose point of view was being outnumbered in a system of voting.

Resolving Conflicts Within the Flock of God

The Book of Acts expresses the work of the Holy Spirit in producing resonance and that of the administrator as a resonator of the intentions of the Holy Spirit to produce wholeness or purity of heart within the individual and the fellowship of believers. The Corinthian correspondence reflects the church and its members in a power struggle between the needs of the individual as over against edification or building up of the corporate fellowship of the church. A spiritual overseer has the responsibility of recognizing the varieties of gifts within the flock of God, appreciating the varieties of service, perceiving the varieties of workings. He must have the grace and compassion, the overview and perception to see that "each is given the manifestation of the Spirit for the common good" (I Corinthians 12:7). All within the fellowship, regardless of the multiplicity of their gifts, are "made to drink of one Spirit." Each has need of the other. Declarations of independence must mature into covenants of interdependence. Attestations of superiority of gifts must be brought under the discipline of the Spirit. No one is expendable and no one is indispensable, but each thrives upon his sense or need for the other. The eye cannot say to the hand, "I have no need of you." The Holy Spirit brings both the voluntary and the involuntary dimensions of the Christian fellowship into mutual coordination. This is the intention of the Holy Spirit as he works through the spiritual administrator of the people of God.

The administrator therefore is primarily responsible for what Kurt Lewin aptly calls "resolving social conflict." He has two possible alternatives for resolving social conflict. He can rely upon the guidance of the Holy Spirit, or he can rely upon cleverness and power politics. First, he can commune with the Holy Spirit in the search for the "new thing" God is seeking to bring forth in the lives of individuals and groups. He searches with prayer in the Spirit for the witness of the Spirit in the new bursts of creativity in the individual and the corporate fellowship. He pays attention to the processes of assimilation of new people, knowing that in receiving strangers and strange ideas he may or may not be entertaining angels unawares. At the same time, he is sensitive both to his own need and that of individuals and small groups to sacrifice the whole Body of Christ for pride, self-elevation, and unvarnished individualism that cares not for community. The red-meat leap for power, prestige, and money is a more vivid temptation for Christians than for pagans. We have so many ways of mistaking it for altruism, prophetic secret, and spiritual excellence.

The writer of the Gospel of Matthew must have had in mind this kind of necessity for resolving social conflict in the early church when he suggested a specific formula as to *how* to resolve social conflict. The first step in that formula is mutual initiative by contending persons. One goes to his brother who has offended him. Open confrontation on a one-to-one basis allows for anger, catharsis of grief, confession of hurt, and appeals for communion and fellowship. However, this does not always resolve the conflict, and the Scriptures suggest that a third person—and this may well be the spiritual overseer—serve as a resonator of the impulses of the Spirit in the bonds of peace. The peacemaker has a blessedness and an identity as a son of God. When one serves in this function, he accepts responsibility for spiritual oversight. But even so, the offending brother is prone not to listen, either to his offended brother or to his peacemaking kinsman in the Spirit. Then and only then can the matter be dealt with in the total reacting power of the church as a whole. The keys of the kingdom are for the unlocking of deadlocked human relationships. When the administrator, by the power of the Holy Spirit, is enabled to bring this to pass, a spirit of prayer and reunion occurs. "For where two or three are gathered in my name, there am I in the midst of them" (Matthew 18:20). This is the promise of Christ.

Social conflict does not always resolve quite so happily, however. The individual offender may refuse to listen to anyone except himself and his own desires. He functions as a Gentile and a tax collector, says the Scripture, and should be considered in the same way. Yet one must remember that Jesus himself had a very different attitude toward Gentiles and tax collectors from that of the Pharisees. He looked upon them with compassion and tenderness, and occasionally one became his disciple. This is still true for the administrator today. Just because a person refuses to listen to anyone does not change his primary status as a person made in the image of God and as one for whom Christ died. Hence the temptation to depersonalize those who will not listen must be offset by "looking to oneself" lest he also be tempted to close his mind and shut his ears to the words of admonition of fellow Christians and to the instruction of the Holy Spirit. Apart from this maintenance of openness, the administrator will perceive the "Gentile and tax collector" as a dog or some other less-than-human creature. (The author is aware of the form critics' analysis of the passage in Matthew 18:50–20 on which the foregoing interpretation of the function of the administrator in relation to the Holy Spirit has been made. The suggestion that this passage was formulated by the later church groups as a part of the Scripture serves to underscore rather than to negate the conclusions drawn here. If these were the remembered interpretations of the mind of Christ by later Christians, then it means that a Christian community had gone to work and made specific great principles which, even if they were not the exact words of Jesus, nevertheless attest to the continuing work of the Holy Spirit with the contemporary administrators of churches in providing them a tested way of dealing with conflict in the fellowship of believers.)

A second, more mundane method of resolving social conflict is an option for the administrator. When he himself ceases to listen to anyone but himself, he yet has the responsibility of tending the flock. Then he must resort to the use of cleverness and maneuvering in order to accomplish his own ends. In turn, those whom he has striven to understand and to listen to become clever to the extent of their ability. They resort to maneuvers or "games" with one another. In political life today this is known as power politics. Stephen Potter has dealt with this in his book *Three-upmanship: The Theory and Practice of Games-manship.*[10] More recently, Eric Berne has treated the ways in which people both consciously and unconsciously avoid openness and intimacy with each other. When they are together either at work or in social gatherings "life is taken up with playing games." Not all games are bad, he says, but the more nearly disturbed and sick the person gets, the more deadly the games become. The stakes are high and the game is played for keeps.[11]

The modern pastor cannot be too much of a purist about "not using power" in human relationships. The "Gentiles and tax gatherers," even within today's institutional church, seem to understand *only* this kind of language. The struggle of the soul of the Christian administrator is to know *when* to use power in behalf of his organization and *how* to avoid "lording it over" those to whom he is called as "an example unto the flock."

Activating Divine Conviction From Within

The Fourth Gospel speaks of the ministry of the Holy Spirit as Counselor. In his coming, he *convinces* the world of sin, of righteousness, and of judgment. The Holy Spirit is concerned with *convincing,* not merely with sin, righteousness, or judgment. This ministry of convincing goes on both *within* and *between* individuals. The confession of sin, the comfort of having done justly, loved mercy, and walked humbly with God, and the gift of sober judgment cannot be pasted on, nailed on, or beaten into a person. The covenant of Jeremiah speaks clearly about the way of the Lord in putting his law *within* us and writing his law upon our hearts. Our neighbor does not have to teach, cajole, or corner us to tell us, "know the Lord." The Holy Spirit does just this, and the true administrator is his witness as he patiently waits for people to come to a clear realization of their own faults. An externally forced apology may bring a socially conforming expression of "Excuse me" or "I'm sorry." Instructions from the leader of a group may be obediently followed. But these are not even near equivalents to the inner sense of conviction for which the Holy Spirit seeks. The administrator grieves the Holy Spirit when he seeks to force insight upon an individual or group. This might produce conformity, but it will not produce conviction.

Therefore, a member of the Body of Christ can live in such separation that deception and breaches of the covenant of openness take the place of honest expression of even negative feelings. Techniques of denial can become so deeply rooted that the person or group may be sincere in their words to their fellowman but extremely deceptive of themselves. This is the beginning of pathology in an individual or group. Not only can the administrator grieve the Holy Spirit, but any member of the flock of God may be at the same time very sincere with his fellowman and actually deceiving or lying to the Holy Spirit. This was the plight of Ananias and Sapphira. Their deception was not with the fellowship of believers in keeping back a part of the proceeds of the land. Peter put his finger on the problem when he said that Satan had filled the heart of Ananias "to lie to the Holy Spirit." He told him: "You have not lied to men but to God" (Acts 5:4b).

In our pietistic need for sweetness and light, emotional warmth and tenderness in human relationships, we would like to edit this gruesome chapter from the Book of Acts.

We would like to move it over to the Old Testament and say that this was a primitive conception of God, that a man and his wife should both die over one insignificant piece of property. But in the New Testament it is. The man and his wife "agreed together to tempt the Spirit of the Lord." The forces of illness, deterioration, and death set in, not when men lie to each other, but when a person lies to himself and to the Spirit of God. Ananias and Sapphira had no place to hide from the truth about themselves. To see the whole truth about ourselves at once would kill us.

I am sure that the stereotypes of administration which we reject so thoroughly are related to the problems of money raising and property holding. From the conflicts over the allocation of the annual budgets of churches, denominations, and ecumenical organizations to the purchase or sale of church property, to the problems of open occupancy for people of all races—the deceit of and resistance to the Holy Spirit's leadership exact their tolls on the bodily structures of administrators and those whom they lead alike. For example, the denominational executive who goes to his annual "allocation of funds" meeting does so with a prayer for freedom from cynicism. The future of his agency depends on this moment, not on the willingness of the populace to give money, but upon the kinds of pressure groups that arise to allocate the money one way or another. He may have spent much of his nights as well as his days negotiating with "the right people" in order to assure that his school, commission, or set of projects is properly interpreted in the decision-making committee. The strain of this kind of political maneuvering on a sensitive and pastorally oriented administrator is immense. The recent volume, *Preachers in Purgatory,* documents the wear and tear upon the lives of ministers and their families in the fray of such crises. I myself have counseled with ministers amid such "purgatories" as depressions, heart attacks, paranoid reactions, and threatened suicides. The data on these are intensely personal, and living people would be hurt by the publication here or elsewhere of the toll upon the health of administrators within the organized life of the churches.[12]

The psychophysiological unity of man has been studied carefully by such authorities as Flanders Dunbar and O. S. English, and practice of comprehensive medicine today reveals the mysterious ways in which fear, hatred, and deception are translated into bodily reactions that may functionally disable a person. If emotions that disable a person are sustained over a long period of time, the actual tissues themselves are damaged. Without adequate medical attention, the person may actually die. Harold Wolff, the late professor of neurology at Cornell Medical School, studied prisoners of war who were "cut off" from their lasting communities of fellow soldiers, family, and home and found that they would die without some ray of hope for their lives. Closely related to this is the problem of suicide.[13] Consequently, the administrator of the life of the church must take heed to his own health. Thorough medical attention and private consultative resources provide the administrator help here. He needs an "overseer" himself.

The contemporary administrator cares for people's lives, not simply by performing acts of kindness and spreading cheer. He deals with matters of life and death as he studies and treats the "living human documents" of people's interaction with each other in the Body of Christ. Obedience and sensitivity to the tutelage of the Holy Spirit

are exchanged for the cleverness and cunningness of human manipulation. The administrator must be constantly
aware that what immature and insensitive people mistake
for harmless games can indeed be *deadly* games. Ananias
and Sapphira agreed together to remain uncommitted and
at the same time to appear as if they were committed.
They apparently thought this a harmless gambit. The end
result was death.

The existential psychologists have taught much about
the open and the closed self, the authentic existence and
the unauthentic existence. The Apostle Paul speaks of
authenticity in terms of living in relation to "the Lord who
is the Spirit" with an unveiled face. This calls for renunciation of "disgraceful, underhanded ways" and a refusal
"to practice cunning or to tamper with God's word, but by
the open statement of the truth . . . [to] commend
ourselves to every man's conscience in the sight of God"
(II Corinthians 4:2). The psychoanalytic schools of psychology have given us clinical studies of the ways in which
people deceive, not only their neighbor, but themselves.
The mechanisms of repression, denial, isolation, projec-
tion, reaction formation, and displacement elaborate the
ingenuity of the human heart to deceive itself. Self-decep-
tion and an inner loss of integrity before the Lord who is
Spirit are the roots of relationships of distrust between
people.

Genuine encounter with God through his act of redemption in Jesus Christ and his continuing revelation of
himself in the Holy Spirit optimumly brings a person into
authentic relationship to God, to himself, and to his
neighbor. Simply "filling the position" and "playing the
role" are the negative counterparts of this trustworthiness.
Credibility gaps appear when expediency and phoniness

replace Christian candor. The administrator of the people of God has his work cut out for him. He may mobilize the administrative structures so as to heal and not merely manipulate people. He has childish, immature, and hard-hearted people who play games with each other. However harmless the games may be and however much the partici-pants play hide-and-go-seek with each other, hazards are at hand into which they can fall to destruction. Through the power of the Holy Spirit he must catch them before they do. He knows that he does not always succeed. He is grieved when he fails. But his personal grief cannot be to him a burden of guilt. Each man has to bear his own burden in matters of life and death, also. But the adminis-trator of the flock of God takes heed to himself and to all the flock, in which the Holy Spirit has made him a guardian, to care for and tend the church of God, which Christ obtained with his own blood.

Yet what has been called "executive loneliness" is more of a reality than it need be. The administrator who perceives himself as a cooperative laborer together with God through the Holy Spirit does not do so in isolation. The great function of the Holy Spirit is to lead him and to provide him with companionship. At the same time, he does this through the organism of the very imperfect church itself. Here are resourceful people who have much to offer him if he only sensed his own need for help too.

Notes

Chapter 1—The Holy Spirit and the Expansion of Consciousness

1. Huston Smith, "Do Drugs Have Religious Import?," *The Journal of Philosophy*, LXI, No. 18 (October 1, 1964), 528.
2. William James, *The Varieties of Religious Experience* (New York: Modern Library, 1902), pp. 378–79.
3. Gardner Murphy, *Personality: A Biosocial Approach to Origins and Structure* (New York: Harper & Bros., 1947), p. 921.
4. Walter N. Pahnke, M.D., "Drugs and Mysticism: An Analysis of the Relationship Between Psychedelic Drugs and the Mystical Consciousness" (unpublished Ph.D. dissertation, Harvard University, Cambridge, Mass., 1963), p. 242. A summary of this research is found in the article by Walter N. Pahnke, M.D., Ph.D., and William A. Richards, S.T.M., "Implications of LSD and Experimental Mysticism," *The Journal of Religion and Health*, V, No. 3 (July, 1966), 175–208.
5. Sidney Cohen, M.D., and Keith S. Ditman, M.D., "Prolonged Adverse Reactions to Lysergic Acid Diethylamid,"

Archives of General Psychiatry, VIII (May, 1963), 71–76.

6. Pahnke and Richards, *op. cit.,* p. 202.
7. Erik H. Erikson, "Youth: Fidelity and Diversity," *Daedalus: Journal of the American Academy of Arts and Sciences,* XCI, No. 1 (Winter, 1962), 14.
8. S. Spafford Ackerly, "Late Adolescence: A Lying Fallow Period of Consolidation," in *Conditio Humana,* Walter von Baeyer and Richard M. Griffith, eds. (Berlin: Springer Verlag, 1966), pp. 5–13.
9. Leland P. Bradford, Jack R. Gibb, and Kenneth D. Benne (eds.), *Training Group Theory and Laboratory Method* (New York: John Wiley & Sons, 1964), p. 117.
10. Richard P. Marsh, "Meaning and the Mind Drugs," *ETC.* (Special Issue on the Psychedelic Experience), XXII, No. 4 (December, 1965), 414–15.
11. Eric Berne, *Games People Play* (New York: Grove Press, 1964).
12. Smith, *op. cit.,* p. 530.
13. Pahnke, *op. cit.,* pp. 175–208
14. Harold Fallding, "The Source and Burden of Civilization Illustrated in the Use of Alcohol," *The Quarterly Journal of Studies on Alcohol,* XXV, No. 4 (December, 1964), 718–19.
15. R. C. Zaehner, *Mysticism: Sacred and Profane* (New York: Oxford University Press, 1961), p. 106.
16. S. I. Hayakawa, "The Quest for Instant Satori," *ETC.* (A Review of General Semantics), XXII, No. 4 (December, 1965), 392.
17. *Ibid.*
18. Pahnke and Richards, *op. cit.,* p. 182.
19. Esther M. Harding, *Journey into Self* (New York: Longmans, Green & Co., 1956), p. 259.
20. *Ibid.,* p. 268.

21. Nathaniel Hawthorne, "The Celestial Railroad," *Mosses from an Old Manse* (Philadelphia: Henry Altemus, 1846), pp. 207–30.
22. Henlee Barnette, *The Holy Spirit and Christian Ethics* (Nashville: The Christian Life Commission, 1954), p. 6.
23. Sidney Cohen, *The Beyond Within* (New York: Atheneum Publishers, 1965), pp. 231–32.
24. Anton Boisen, *The Exploration of the Inner World* (New York: Harper & Bros., 1952), p. 61.
25. Anton Boisen, *Out of the Depths* (New York: Harper & Bros., 1960).

Chapter 2—Nonverbal Communication and the Help of the Holy Spirit

1. William Sanday and Arthur C. Headlam, *A Critical and Exegetical Commentary on the Epistle to the Romans* (New York: Charles Scribner's Sons, 1896), pp. 212–13.
2. "Dr. Mead Scores Degree Criteria," *The New York Times,* July 18, 1965.
3. Robert Cohen, "Language and Behavior," *American Scientist,* XLIX (1961), 507.
4. Frederick Perls, Ralph Hefferline, and Paul Goodman, *Gestalt Therapy* (New York: Julian Press, 1951), p. 419.
5. Alfred Korzybski, *Science and Sanity* (3rd ed.; Lakeville, Conn.: The Institute of General Semantics, 1948), p. 417.
6. Jacques Hadamard, *Psychology of Invention in the Mathematical Field* (Princeton: Princeton University Press, 1949), p. 118.
7. Amos N. Wilder, *The Language of the Gospel: Early Christian Rhetoric* (New York: Harper & Row, 1964), p. 32.
8. Jacob Moreno, *Who Shall Survive?* (2nd ed.; New York: Beacon House, 1960), p. 81

9. Ralph Turner, "Role Taking, Role Standpoint, and Reference-Group Behavior," in *Role Theory: Concepts and Research,* B. J. Biddle and Edwin J. Thomas, eds. (New York: John Wiley & Sons, 1966), p. 157.

10. Albert Camus, *The Fall* (New York: Alfred A. Knopf, 1960), pp. 88–90.

11. Robert Frost, "Revelation," *The Poems of Robert Frost* (New York: Modern Library, 1946), p. 23.

12. Leland E. Hinsie and Jacob Shatzky, *Psychiatric Dictionary* (New York: Oxford University Press, 1953), p. 467.

13. David C. McClelland, "Religious Overtones in Psychoanalysis," in *The Ministry and Mental Health,* Hans Hoffmann, ed. (New York: Association Press, 1960), p. 49.

14. *Ibid.,* p. 63.

15. William T. Blackstone, "The Status of God-Talk," *Journal for the Scientific Study of Religion,* V, No. 3 (Fall, 1966), 365.

16. D. T. Suzuki, Erich Fromm, and Richard De Martino, *Zen Buddhism and Psychoanalysis* (New York: Harper & Bros., 1960), p. 127.

17. *Ibid.*

18. Jurgen Ruesch and Weldon Kees, *Nonverbal Communication* (Berkeley: University of California Press, 1956), pp. 16–17.

19. Eduard Schweizer, "Lord in All Seriousness," *The Pulpit,* XXVII, No. 10 (November, 1966), 25.

20. Jean Piaget, *The Language and Thought of the Child* (New York: Meridian Books, 1955), p. 33.

21. Harry Stack Sullivan, *The Interpersonal Theory of Psychiatry* (New York: W. W. Norton & Co., 1953), pp. 84–85.

22. *Ibid.,* p. 185.

23. Suzuki, Fromm, and De Martino, *op. cit.,* p. 129.

Chapter 3—The Holy Spirit and the Ministry of Articulation

1. News item in the *Courier Journal and Louisville Times,* February 26, 1967.
2. Dietrich Bonhoeffer, *No Rusty Swords* (New York: Harper & Row, 1965), p. 20.
3. Edmund Husserl, *Ideas: General Introduction to Pure Phenomenology,* trans. W. R. Boyce Gibson (New York: Collier Books, 1962), p. 194.
4. Helmut Thielicke, *Theological Ethics* (Philadelphia: Fortress Press, 1966), I, 650.
5. Gabriel Marcel, *Homo Viator: Introduction to a Metaphysics of Hope* (New York: Harper & Row, 1962), p. 39.
6. H. Wheeler Robinson, *The Christian Experience of the Holy Spirit* (New York: Harper & Bros., 1928), p. 4.
7. "Defiance in Hungary," news item in *The New York Times,* October 31, 1961.

Chapter 4—The New Morality: A Psychological and Theological Critique

1. Joseph A. Fletcher, *Situation Ethics: The New Morality* (Philadelphia: Westminster Press, 1966).
2. *Ibid.,* p. 26.
3. *Ibid.*
4. William Temple, *Christian Life and Faith* (London: SCM, 1954), p. 97.
5. Fletcher, *op. cit.,* p. 51.
6. Temple, *op. cit.,* p. 91.
7. Paul Tillich, *Systematic Theology* (Chicago: University of Chicago Press, 1963), III, 292.

8. Thomas Aquinas, *Summa Theologiae,* I–II, 90, 1; II–III, 50, 1 and 1.

9. Eric C. Rust, "The Holy Spirit, Nature and Man" (unpublished manuscript), p. 1.

10. Kurt Lewin, *Principles of Topological Psychology* (New York: McGraw-Hill, 1936), pp. 13–16.

11. Gardner Murphy, *Personality: A Biosocial Approach to Origins and Structure* (New York: Basic Books, Inc., 1947; reprinted with a new preface, 1966), pp. 867–68.

12. *Ibid.,* p. 882.

13. *Ibid.,* p. 881.

14. *Ibid.,* p. 884.

15. *Ibid.,* pp. 888–89.

16. *Ibid.,* p. 890.

17. Andras Angyal, *Neurosis and Treatment: A Holistic Approach* (New York: John Wiley & Sons, 1965), pp. 187–89.

18. Murphy, *loc. cit.*

19. Telford Taylor, *The Breaking Wave: The Second World War in the Summer of 1940* (New York: Simon & Schuster, 1967).

20. Robert Bolt, *A Man For All Seasons* (New York: Random House, 1960), p. 140.

Chapter 5—The Holy Spirit in an Age of Administration

1. William H. Whyte, Jr., *The Organization Man* (New York: Doubleday & Co., 1957), p. 14.

2. John D. Maguire, "Where Can God Be Found?," *Christianity and Crisis,* XXV, No. 21 (December 13, 1965), 1.

3. Seward Hiltner, *A Preface to Pastoral Theology* (New York: Abingdon Press, 1958).

4. Reuel Howe, *The Miracle of Dialogue* (Greenwich, Conn.: Seabury Press, 1963), p. 106.

5. Gabriel Marcel, *The Mystery of Being,* Vol. I of *Reflection and Mystery* (Chicago: Henry Regnery, 1950), p. 127.

6. Erik Erikson, *Identity and the Life Cycle* (New York: International Universities Press, 1960), pp. 89–90.

7. Andras Angyal, *Neurosis and Treatment* (New York: John Wiley & Sons, 1965), pp. 45–48.

8. *Ibid.*

9. *Ibid.,* pp. 45–58.

10. Stephen Potter, *Three-upmanship: The Theory and Practice of Gamesmanship* (New York: Holt, Rinehart and Winston, 1962).

11. Eric Berne, *The Structure and Dynamics of Organizations and Groups* (Philadelphia: J. B. Lippincott, 1963). A more popular treatment of this is found in his best-seller, *Games People Play* (New York: Grove Press, 1964), pp. 63–65.

12. Lester Mondale, *Preachers in Purgatory* (Boston: Beacon Press, 1966).

13. Harold G. Wolff, Charter Day Address of the Society of the New York Hospital, May 8, 1956.

DATE DUE